SPIRIT OF
CHINA

SPIRIT OF
CHINA

A PHOTOGRAPHIC JOURNEY OF THE PEOPLE, CULTURE AND HISTORY

GILL DAVIES

Bath New York Singapore Hong Kong Cologne Delhi Melbourne

First published by Parragon in 2008

Parragon
Queen Street House
4 Queen Street
Bath BA1 1HE, UK

Designed, produced, and packaged by
Stonecastle Graphics Limited

Text by Gill Davies
Designed by Paul Turner and Sue Pressley
Edited by Philip de Ste. Croix
Picture research by Nick Freeth

ISBN 978-1-4075-2515-0

Printed in China

Page 1: *Here, cloaked in mist in Hunan province, is the beautiful Zhangjiajie mountain and national park where over 3000 jagged sandstone pillars and peaks soar above ravines, caves, gorges, natural bridges, streams, pools, and waterfalls — all surrounded by thick forest.*

Pages 2-3: *Marco Polo described Hangzhou as the world's most beautiful and magnificent city. Water gleams everywhere as the city lies on the lower reaches of Qiantang River, close to the Chang delta and at the southern tip of China's Grand Canal: glittering West Lake was a favorite imperial retreat.*

CONTENTS

Introduction

Page 6

土水火木金

INTRODUCTION

China is an amazing nation and, from a western perspective, something of an enigma. For millennia it was a very secret place, first revealing some of its vast territories to western eyes when reached by pilgrims or traders who traveled along the Silk Road that stretched some 5000 miles (8000km) over land and sea and linked Europe with the eastern part of Africa. China opened its doors just a fraction wider when an Italian associate of Francis of Assisi, a Franciscan monk, John de Plano Carpini, was sent by Pope Innocent IV as an envoy to the East in 1245. Some 20 years later, Marco Polo arrived at the Chinese court from where he brought back to Europe fascinating tales of magical Cathay. However, then China slammed the door firmly shut again in 1400 when foreigners were denied entry. In due course envoys were permitted into the country provided they were representatives of royal courts, and treaty ports helped trade to flourish.

A culture of invention

China's highly advanced culture has introduced a phenomenal number of wonderful discoveries to the western world including many significant inventions — some of which changed our civilization — such as gunpowder, printing, papermaking and paper currency, the abacus, stirrups, the seismometer, porcelain, silk, and the compass.

This is a truly ancient place. Some of the earliest evidence of human civilization has been found in China. As well as the fossilized remains of the renowned Peking man, *Homo erectus*, discovered in the 1920s in the Zhoukoudian cave in today's suburban Beijing — a hominid ancestor who dates back some 250,000-600,000 years in China — there are also the remains of Yuanmou Man and Lantian Man who both lived between 1 million and 750,000 years ago. Both of these are also attributed to the *Homo erectus* species. The earliest flower fossils have been found here too and so it comes as no surprise to realize that one of the greatest world civilizations eventually developed here — some 7000 to 8000 years ago. China's written records date back 4000 years or so and it joins ancient Egypt, Babylon, and India as the cradle of one of the world's supreme ancient civilizations. China can boast the longest consistently used written language system in history.

Great philosophers and teachers like Confucius have contributed to the way the world thinks and how we understand our place in the universe. Chinese astronomers were the first to record a solar prominence (an observation inscribed on a tortoise shell), a meteor shower in 2133 BC and the earliest verified solar eclipse recorded during the Shang Dynasty in 1217 BC.

From astronomy we pass to astrology — and the basis for the five sections in this book. Many aspects of life in China are viewed as being part of the cycle of creation and decay embodied in the five elements — earth, water, fire, wood, and metal. It impacts upon many facets of Chinese culture including music, medicine, military strategy, and martial arts. The elements are associated with the planets, parts of the body, seasons of the year, lifecycles, the five senses, livestock, heavenly animals (such as dragons and white tigers), body organs, emotions, color, and direction.

Above: *Many Chinese temples have gold decorative features.*

Opposite: *The cityscape glitters at night beyond Hong Kong's impressive Convention and Exhibition Center.*

The five Chinese elements

Accordingly, this exploration of China uses the five elements as its 'backbone.' The first to be considered here is *Earth* and this provides an opportunity to look at the huge variety of terrain in China, plus the people living there — and the animals that inhabit these contrasting landscapes. China exults in jagged snowy mountain peaks in the north where Everest rises, lush jungle, rock-strewn deserts like the Gobi, warm beaches, turquoise lakes, tiers of paddy strips wrapped around misty mountain contours, and sand dunes glittering with frost in winter.

The second section, *Water*, follows the flow of seas, rivers, lakes, and waterfalls that sparkle in many a different landscape. It discovers ports, islands, fishing communities, and creatures that flourish in these domains.

Fire represents inspiration, excitement, and creativity, so here art, literature, theater, calligraphy, cuisine, inventions, and religion are explored. So too are dragons, kites, fireworks, carnivals, and parades — and how heat engendered by fire helps to create that quintessential product of China — beautiful porcelain.

Our fourth element is *Wood* so trees and bamboo forests are revealed, together with the secretive creatures of the forest. In China, timber and its products are used to create wooden pagodas, furniture, musical instruments, and paper. We shall discover how paper is folded and cut here so effectively to make a dazzling variety of products from glimmering lanterns to opera masks and amazing suits of armor.

Finally we look at how *Metal* is smelted and how tools chop wood in the process of engineering and construction.

So buildings rise, cities grow, bridges bestride the water, and roads loop over the landscape to create vital links. This is an opportunity to explore the Bronze Age and the Terra-Cotta Army, the vibrant ports of Shanghai and Hong Kong, cities like Nanjing and Imperial Beijing, as well as the Great Wall and the beautiful temples, tombs, pagodas, vast statues, palaces, and gardens that create their own special magic in this amazing nation.

City streets still throng with bicycles but now more cars are appearing as China surges headlong into the modern age with brilliant skyscrapers thrusting to the skies and technical expertise exploding in many directions. For 600 years or so, the Forbidden City in Beijing denied entry to anyone other than Imperial Court members, but times have changed rapidly in the last 20 years. Now there is a Starbucks serving coffee within those once-so-mysterious walls, an all-too-obvious symbol of how modern China is now embracing the culture of globalization.

Today, China is growing and changing at an incredible rate, moving forward from its 5000-year history to become a modern nation at the forefront of commerce, manufacture, industry, science, and sport. Its huge population of some 1,321,851,000 people is the largest of any country in the world. This is a land of imaginative and inventive people who, moved by the spirit of who they are and the world around them, have long expressed their love of nature and their religious ideals through creativity and innovation. China is home to an incredibly rich and varied heritage encompassing calligraphy, art, architecture, medicine, philosophy … and much, much more.

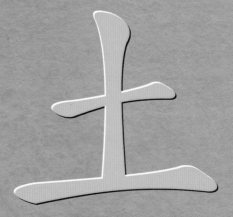

EARTH

China is big! Correction … China is very big! When unfurling a map or spinning a globe, it is hard to conceive that this vast area comprises just one nation, and not a continent. It is the greatest country found entirely within Asia, the fourth largest in the world and is home to over 1.3 billion people, more than one-fifth of the globe's population.

Left: Clouds drift between green-mantled peaks and crags in Lushan National Park.

A land of contrasts

Of course, as the old adage protests, size isn't everything, but China in a way is everything: it is like an exciting encyclopedia in its own right, a compendium of many thousands of amazing facets. There are wildly different landscapes from soaring mountains to bamboo forests, from vivacious bustling cities to the calm of a desert lying silent under the stars, or the shifting silver gleam of paddy fields.

Its history includes a period of many centuries when China was unified as a large empire ruled over by a succession of dynasties. This period began in 221 BC and survived until AD 1912.

This big knuckle of land occupies some 3,700,593sq miles (9,584,492km²) and has a land border of 13,759 miles (22,143km) that butts against the frontiers of 14 other countries: Afghanistan, Bhutan, India, Kazakhstan, North Korea, Kyrgyzstan, Laos, Mongolia, Myanmar, Nepal, Pakistan, Russia, Tajikistan, and Vietnam. China's coastline extends about 8700 miles (14,000km) from its border with North Korea in the north to Vietnam in the south. This landmass is washed on its eastern and southern flanks by Korea Bay, the Yellow Sea, the East China Sea, and the South China Sea.

China consists of 22 provinces, five autonomous regions, and four municipalities. Here swirling rice-growing terraces wrap the mountainsides like the contours on a relief map. Lowlands and plains sprawl in the east while in the north there are heavily populated alluvial plains and grasslands that stretch to the edges of the Inner Mongolian plateau. The northeast has dense coniferous forests where Asiatic black bears roam. The northwest is home to a great alluvial plain as well as high plateaus and amazing deserts — the ever-expanding Gobi and the Takla Makan where Bactrian camels are found.

The lowest point in China is the Turfan Depression (Turpan Pendi) in the northwest, one of the few places in the world set lower than sea level, lying as it is at 508ft (155m) down below, with a salt lake nestled in the depression. Once, long ago, this was a strategic point on the Silk Road, where travelers, merchants, and monks would pause on the long route to the west.

The mighty Himalayas flank China's southwest boundaries, soaring skyward like jagged white teeth. Meanwhile, as a dramatic contrast, there are steamy tropical jungles in the deep south where tigers prowl — and giant pandas gaze out through their black patched eyes in the bamboo forests of central and western China.

Distances are vast here: a journey from west to east would mean sweeping across some 3231 miles (5200km). China from north to south measures over 3418 miles (5500km). Time zones change across the east-west axis (although the whole of China operates to a single standard time — GMT + 8 hours) — just as climates do from north to south, for while the north is being buffeted by sharp winter blizzards, spring is being welcomed in the south.

Left: The stunning razor-sharp peaks of the Himalayas, the youngest mountains on Earth, rise into the clouds at the southwest edge of China.

Right: Near Guilin city, glistening river waters are encircled by green hillsides, cliffs, caves, and dramatic karst rock formations that rise from the verdant plain — creating the impression of a skyline of crooked dragon's teeth.

Right: Terraced ricefields near Guilin spiral up the steep hillsides to the mountain tops, looking rather like fingerprint whorls as they create a unique curving pattern, their edges often shining silver with water. Many such intricate terraces were built during the Ming Dynasty, about 500 years ago.

Above: Zhangjiajie National Forest Park has an incredible landscape of towering steep peaks and contorted rocks — the inspiration for many Chinese paintings. There are spectacular caves here too, while golden pheasant, rhesus monkeys, giant salamanders, and musk deer may be found among lush vegetation in this unique habitat.

Weather: all the extremes

A country this large and with such varied terrain inevitably experiences a great variety of weather patterns and China's climate ranges from desert to tropical to sub-Arctic zones.

The northern zone (where Beijing is located) enjoys summer daytime temperatures of over 86°F (30°C) but the winters are freezing cold. Dropping south to the central zone (where Shanghai lies) the weather is temperate and continental with very hot summers and cold winters. In the south, however, the weather is subtropical with very hot summers and mild winters.

Sometimes the weather can impose especially difficult conditions as drought and dust storms, which are often experienced inland. Also, typhoons regularly batter the coastal regions with so much ferocity that towns can be flooded and mass evacuations may be necessary as winds gust up to 165mph (265kph). But there are balmy times too when peach trees blossom and spring is celebrated in many local festivals.

Earthquakes and volcanoes

China's land mass straddles one of the most active seismic regions in the world and has been subject to many destructive earthquakes. In 1556, the Great China Earthquake took more lives than any other quake ever, when a huge tremor estimated to measure from 8.0 to 8.3 on the Richter scale sent vast shock waves radiating out from Hausien in central China's Shanxi province, devastating 98 counties and eight provinces — and, in the process, killing some 830,000 people.

More recently, in 1975, a 7.3 magnitude earthquake struck Haicheng (in Liaoning province in northeast China) but due to early warnings and prompt evacuation, while damage to property was considerable, few lives were lost. However, when a massive earthquake struck the busy city of Tangshan (just east of Beijing in northern China) in July 1976 with an 8.0 magnitude, a 5 mile (8km) section of the fault line moved 5ft (1.5m) northward, tipping downward and upward at its extremes. The quake was so strong that people were simply tossed into the air while homes, factories, bridges, roads, and railroads collapsed. More than 240,000 people may have died, with some 500,000 injured. This was the second worst earthquake in recorded history.

There are some 30 volcano groups and a thousand or so volcanoes in China, mainly located in the north and northeast. Experts warn that the volcanoes at Changbai mountains are potentially dangerous despite their centuries of dormancy. Baitoushan on the China-Korean border was last active in 1702. There are also mud volcanoes, which consist of huge mounds of mud slurry raised up by seismic activity, and 36 of these have erupted on the northern slope of Mount Tianshan in northwest China.

China's countless extinct volcanoes include a massive group of volcanic cones in the Great Plain where natural gas and petroleum can be seen spewing out of the craters in as many as 60 eruptions per minute.

Left: *Tianchi Lake, at the top of the Baekdu Mountain in northeastern China, is the world's highest volcanic crater lake. China's many extinct and dormant volcanoes have not erupted for centuries.*

Below: *Heavy storm clouds sweep over the darkened outline of mountains in Tibet — a wild, remote and often barren landscape that is sometimes referred to as the Roof of the World.*

profusion of plants and wildlife

China's abundant natural resources and vast wild landscapes provide habitats for more than 4500 species of vertebrates including 1244 species of bird, 430 mammals, 208 amphibians, 350 reptiles, and 2300 fishes — one of the greatest varieties of wildlife species found in a single nation. There are many rare endemic creatures including golden monkeys, Chinese alligators, crested ibises, and the giant pandas. Here too are white-lipped deer, brown-eared pheasants, Chinese river dolphins, Asian elephants, snow leopards, and tigers. Of the 15 species of crane in the world, nine live in China.

In the more isolated areas there are incredibly varied plants and animals — so much so that almost every major plant found in the tropical and temperate zones of the northern hemisphere is found here — some 7000 species of woody plants including 2800 timber trees and more than 300 species of gymnosperms (a group of woody plants including seed ferns, conifers, and cycads). China boasts 650 of the 800 known varieties of azalea and has 390 varieties of primrose and about 230 gentians. The 400 varieties of the tree peony originated in Shandong province.

Ancient and rare ginkgo or maidenhair trees *(Ginkgo biloba)* have been tended and preserved by Chinese monks for over a thousand years. These trees are so old that often they are called 'living fossils' as it is not clear if uncultivated groups of ginkgos can still be found in the wild. They have excellent resistance to disease and attack by insects, growing aerial roots and sprouting again to attain their great longevity. It is claimed that some specimens of this tree are over 2500 years old and a 3000-year-old ginkgo has been reported in Shandong province.

Endangered plant species include the scaly-barked and scaly-coned Yin shan pine trees *(Cathaya argyrophylla)* that cling to steep narrow slopes and which are descended from the extinct species of *Cathaya* that grew on Earth some ten to 30 million years ago. China's many beautiful flowers include gorgeous camellias; the rare yellow *Camellia chrysantha* or *Camellia nitidissima* flourishes in the moist forests of Guangxi, a region in the south. China is home to 46 species of conifers, 33 camellias, 63 hollies, about 300 species of native fern, 31 magnolias, 66 orchids, and 46 rhododendron species. There are 58 species (21 endemic) of iris in China, including stunning white ones. More than 574 forest or wildlife natural reserves have been established to help protect and conserve rare and endangered species — and to reintroduce some extinct ones.

Above: *Slate-colored gray cranes tiptoe over the snow — the Huang River estuary is visited annually by some four million birds, including large numbers of gray cranes.*

Above: *The regal gaze of the rare snow leopard.*

Right: *There may be only around 250 wild elephants in China.*

Left: *Pink and white magnolia blossom heralds spring: this tree evolved before bees did, so the flowers encourage pollination by beetles instead.*

Top: *Bright emerald* Ginkgo biloba *leaves: the plant's ancient ancestry earned its description as a 'living fossil.'*

Above: *A delicate camellia bloom:* Camellia sinensis *leaves and leaf buds are used in China to produce tea.*

Plains, grasslands, and plateaus

In the northeastern highland region, the great plateau of Central Asia covers some 1,000,000sq miles (2,600,000km²) divided (both politically and geographically) by the Gobi Desert into Mongolia and Inner Mongolia — the latter being an autonomous region of China.

Flat or rolling grasslands include the southwestern uplands of the Da Hinggan mountains, which are located in the northeast of Inner Mongolia. Their eastern slopes drop steeply to the northeast China plain. The grasslands northwest of the mountains here suffer icy cold winters as they are blasted by the prevailing winds while cold air is sucked down from the heights of central Asia. In the northeast, large grasslands spread inland from the coastal hills toward the forests of southern Siberia — warm in summer but cold and windblown during the winter months.

Set in China's Sichuan province, on the eastern edge of the Tibetan Plateau, are the Ruoergai marshes (also known as Zoigê Marsh), ranked among the world's largest high-altitude wetlands with about 3860sq miles (10,000km²) of peat bogs — plus sedge marshes, meadows, lakes, and wet grasslands where rare and endemic alpine plant species still survive. The odd low hill rises from the flat landscape while patches of drier grassland are scattered here and there. This marshy expanse — that is the source of the great Chang and Huang Rivers — is home to around 50,000 people, mostly Tibetans who still lead a traditional pastoral lifestyle, caring for vast herds of grazing sheep, yaks, horses, and goats.

Inner Mongolia

The Inner Mongolia autonomous region of China is the third largest administrative district. Here the high tableland features plateaus and dry short-grass steppes. The Han people who live here were traditionally nomadic, traveling with their sheep and goats but now they farm, growing grain — wheat and oats — and vegetables. In Inner Mongolia some areas have been irrigated and sugar beets and oilseeds are cultivated. Natural resources include coal, copper,

fluorite, uranium, gold, and silver. Although the Trans-Mongolian Railway links Ulaanbaatar, the capital of Mongolia, with Russia and the Beijing area and some roads do snake their way across the region, the plateau remains relatively isolated and underdeveloped.

Inner Mongolia's capital city is Hohhot (the Green City). It dates back to the Ming Dynasty, some four centuries ago. Here the oldest temple is Dazhao, boasting a rare 8.2ft (2.5m) high silver Buddha dedicated by the Tibetan Dalai Lama in 1586, and many delicate frescoes and musical instruments. There are carved dragons on the huge golden pillars; a fine pair of iron lions guard the hall.

Important historical sites here include a memorial for the great warrior Genghis Khan (or Emperor Ta Zu [1162-1227], the founder of the Yuan Dynasty). His vast mausoleum on the Ordos Plateau consists of three yurt-shaped palaces with glazed yellow-tiled domes, blue and white walls, and vermilion gates. A palace used by the Khan when he was on his travels is here too.

Visitors to the steppes of Central Asia can still travel and sleep in yurts — portable, felt-covered, wood lattice-framed dwellings once used by nomads. Camels and camel carts also cross the grasslands where, when the traveling day ends, the locals traditionally serve barbecued, boiled, or whole roast lamb, mutton kebabs, and camel hoof — all washed down with tea and milk. Mongolian traditions include folk songs and dances, saber-fights, horseback acrobatics, and horse and camel racing.

Background: *The stony peaks and ridges of the Mongolian desert glow pink as the sun sets.*

Opposite below: *At Karakul Lake in Xinjiang Uygur, it is possible to stay in traditional yurts — latticed-timber, felt-covered dwellings once often used by nomads in this region.*

Below left: *Herds of shaggy, long-haired yaks graze on grasses and lichens on a Mongolian plateau.*

Background: *Horses drink from a Mongolian lake: this stocky native breed is said to be similar to those Genghis Khan would have known. Their strong tail hairs are used to braid ropes and to string violin bows.*

Animals of the plains

The plains are grazed by domestic sheep and goats as well as being home to the Mongolian gazelle, Przewalski's gazelle, and Bactrian camel. The scarlet-faced, brown eared pheasant seeks winter refuge in the shrubs. It has a velvety black head and neck plus stiff white ear coverts that resemble an Edwardian gentleman's bristling mustache. Although endangered, protection does seem to have boosted its numbers recently (see also page 34).

For many centuries Przewalski's horse *(Equus ferus przewalskii)* roamed here too but now hunting and the increase in domestic animals have rung the death knell for many such wild species. The brown-eared pheasant is the sole endemic bird — it winters in lower shrub-grasslands at the forest edges while great bustards and oriental plovers visit to breed on the adjoining plains.

Where China meets Mongolia, the Asiatic wild ass *(Equus hemionus onager)* or onager is found. It is red-brown in summer and yellow-brown in winter and has a black, white-edged stripe snaking along its back. Herds of these sturdy short-legged animals are led by older experienced mares as they graze on sharp, rough plants, like needle grass and speargrass, that would lacerate the mouths of other herbivores. They are scarce now but survive in remote plains, mountains, and deserts.

Opposite above: A great bustard preening: at about 30lb (13.5kg), the huge males are among the heaviest birds flying today.

Opposite below: A small group of Gobi Desert camels: China and Mongolia are setting up a joint wildlife reserve to protect their populations of fast-vanishing wild camels.

Above: Only a few of the truly wild Przewalski's horse survive. They are dun-colored, sometimes with faintly striped legs.

Left: Onagers (Asiatic wild asses) are slightly bigger than donkeys and can run at 43mph (70kph).

The fertile lowlands

The fertile lowlands of China are intensely cultivated; glistening rivers, such as the Huang and the Chang, are edged by vast patchworks of rippling fields in which crops are grown. Grain crops like rice are nurtured intensively in the wetter lowlands and on hill slopes where many a pond is busy with fish, frogs, and ducks.

One of the most exotic Chinese ducks is the male mandarin *(Aix galericulata)* which has orange and red feathers, a white crescent above the eye, black and white belly stripes, orange 'whiskers' and 'sails' on the wings, and a deep maroon breast. Their gorgeous feathers were often used in millinery and these highly decorative birds were frequently depicted in Oriental art. Revered in Far Eastern culture since at least the 400s, they symbolize marital affection and fidelity; pairs were often presented as gifts to newly-weds. Although usually silent, they whistle and call during courtship and very occasionally the male makes a grunting noise like a wild pig. They are not solely water birds — they perch in trees and make their nests in tree holes in densely wooded areas, albeit near to shallow lakes, marshes, or ponds.

Above: *All around Yangshuo in south China farmers plant flooded paddy fields with rice shoots.*

Opposite: *The damp flat terrain of China's lowlands offers good conditions for both rice-growing and wildlife.*

Other wetland creatures

Water buffalo *(Bubalus bubalis)* work as beasts of burden or draft and pack animals, especially in the muddy paddy fields of the south where they are often called the 'living tractor of the East.' They are relied upon for plowing and transportation. Their wide-splayed hoofed feet prevent them from sinking too deeply in the mud and allow them to move about comfortably in wetlands. Slow and ponderous, they produce useful dung that can serve as fertilizer or be dried to make fuel, while their rich creamy milk can be turned into excellent cream and cheese. They are very tame, friendly, and curious, despite their awesome shoulder height of up to 6.2ft (1.5 to 1.9m) and enormous backward-curving horns.

Some 65 mammal, 50 reptile, 45 amphibious animal, and 1040 fish species flourish in China's wetlands, which are also home to over 300 species of birds, including cranes such as the Siberian *(Grus leurogeranus)*, white-naped *(G. vipio)*, hooded *(G. monacha)*, and the common crane *(G. grus)*, many of which visit Yancheng wetlands in Jiangsu province every year to overwinter. The red-crowned crane *(G. japonensis)* is the most numerous representative here, with over 600 of these birds being present. Poyang Lake is another major wintering habitat for the Siberian crane and some 2000 to 3000 individuals fly in each year to overwinter there. Coastal wetlands attract wintering swans.

Some of China's marshes and reedbeds are home to the small, shy Chinese water deer *(Hydropotes inermis)*. They have no antlers but do have tusks, and are sometimes said to have magical powers because of the amazing way their sensitive hearing, smell, and sight can detect any danger. Then they simply 'melt away' into cover. These creatures are excellent swimmers and may swim for several miles to get to river islands.

Rice — staple food

China's most fertile soil lies along the Chang River delta where every available acre of land in the flat watery landscape is cultivated. In the Huang River delta, wetlands occupy an area of 1750sq miles (4500km²) and the wetland soil is so fertile that there may be as many as three harvests per year.

There are 127,400sq miles (33 million hectares) of paddy fields in China where multiple cropping has now been widely adopted to increase annual grain yields — especially in eastern China. In the north wheat is mainly grown whereas the more tropical south, which enjoys plentiful rainfall,

encourages excellent rice crops. This is a staple food that has been grown since ancient times and while actual written evidence of the cultivation of rice in China dates back only 3000 years, archeological evidence suggests that unhusked rice was stored for the military and buried with the dead from Neolithic times onward — from as early as around 9000 BC. Domesticated rice strains were certainly being cultivated by about 6400 BC.

Today rice accounts for more than one fifth of the world's human consumption of calories. While China's flat lowland areas provide ideal conditions for cultivating rice, often the misty hillsides too are woven around with intricate terracing and banks to retain water. Rice growing is labor-intensive at the best of times and is even more so when farmers are working on these high terraces.

Damp zones near rice paddies can be havens for birds and amphibians; grassy areas and ditches near flooded rice paddies are a good place to spot rice frogs, such as the ornate narrow-mouthed frog.

A land of plenty

The flat terrain and generous water resources serve not only the needs of rice growers but also those of city builders and these regions have witnessed the growth of many densely populated industrialized cities. This nation was once known as a land of the hungry, but today few of China's 1.3 billion citizens will go hungry as the economy prospers and industry and manufacture compete with farming for land use. Nowadays, the yearly harvest may well be of garments rather than rice!

Top: *The Chinese regard the brilliantly colored mandarin duck (Aix galericulata) as a symbol of happiness and marital fidelity.*

Left and above: *Encircling hillside rice paddies — near Guilin (left) and at Dragon's Backbone Rice Terraces (above) in Longsheng county —*

Forests and jungle

China has 750 protected national forest areas that together make up a total area of 302,897sq miles (784,500km²); some 8.7 percent of the national territory has been set up to preserve its unique fauna and flora and to serve as a natural resource for scientific research, education, and tourism.

Extensive needle-leaf forests occur in the Greater Hinggan mountains of the northeast with stands of larch, Asian white birch and Scotch pine. In the Lesser Hinggan mountains, Korean pine and Dahurian larch flourish while the Sichuan basin provides a habitat for plants that vary with the elevations — bamboo at the lower levels, deciduous trees and cypresses in the middle, conifers higher up. Farther south, in subtropical Fujian and Zhejiang provinces, broadleaf evergreen forests predominate while China's deep south boasts tropical jungle in the Yunnan basin, which lies on the Tropic of Cancer. This is a most diverse province, which is home to 26 ethnic minority groups and a range of ecosystems from lush tropical jungle to glacial lakes with an equally wide range of plants and animals. Crops can be grown all year in the southern regions here.

On the large island of Hainan, which lies south of mainland China and opposite Vietnam, there are rubber, coconut, and betel nut plantations, lovely waterfalls, dramatic mountain peaks, a plethora of tropical fruits — and jungle where deer, rhesus monkeys, macaques and the not-so-appealing leeches revel in the moist conditions. Jianfengling National Forest park encompasses a vast area of primeval tropical forest where the 4300 animal species include black bears, pangolins, superbly-marked, long-toothed clouded leopards, and black crested gibbons swinging on their incredibly long arms. An impressive sight, standing on a pier built out into the sea, is a new statue of Buddhist holy figure Guan Yin — at 354ft (108m) high this is the world's second tallest figure, higher than the Statue of Liberty. It was formally enshrined in 2005. Inland the hillside villages are home to Li and Miao ethnic groups.

Here grows the Dragon's blood plant, a type of dracaena with red sap that was believed by ancient Chinese herbalists to improve the circulation of the blood, and the red dwarf banana plant as well as many ferns, lianas, figs, and epiphytes scrambling up the trees.

Left: In Zhangjiajie, China's first national park, great pillar-like rocks, shaped by erosion and winter ice, thrust up from a surrounding tapestry of jungle trees and dense foliage.

Above left: A monkey in Jiangsu province where bamboo, fir and pine trees grow.

Above: A river winds past forest and rocky cliffs in Zhejiang province.

Forest animals

There is a well-known Chinese legend of a magical monkey called Sunwukong (which means Monkey King), a kind of mischievous superhero who helped the weak and fought evil with justice. Monkeys are certainly admired in China but sadly they do need protection now as their forest habitats vanish because of intensive logging and agriculture.

The golden snub-nosed monkey is found only in China. There are three species, the Sichuan golden snub-nosed monkey *(Rhinopithecus roxellana)*, Yunnan golden (black-snub-nosed) monkey *(R. bieti)* and Guizhou golden (gray snub-nosed) monkey *(R. brelichi)*, living in large groups (sometimes reaching hundreds in number) in mixed broadleaf and coniferous forests or bamboo jungles on mountains. They are colorful creatures with bright blue faces, golden-orange fur and small upturned snub noses. The males have wart-like growths at the corners of their mouths. They love to nibble away at fruit, tender branches, sprouts,

Above: *Golden snub-nosed monkeys live in China's mountain forests.*

Opposite: *The rare Siberian tiger may soon vanish from China.*

and leaves but are becoming increasingly rare as the forests are cleared for farming, villages, roads, and timber. The last four decades have seen the monkey's Yunnan habitat shrink by a third as pastureland has doubled. Although legally protected by the Chinese government, they are still poached for their beautiful fur, their bones (believed to hold special medicinal powers), and their brains that are considered a culinary delicacy in local cuisine. These beautiful animals are regrettably on the brink of extinction.

The South China tiger

This regal creature — *Panthera tigris amoyensis* — is perhaps the most critically endangered of the five tiger subspecies that survive today. It is the rarest, the most threatened and closest to extinction. Only 40 or so years ago there were reputed to be more than 4000 of these tigers in the wild but, declared pests, they were hunted mercilessly and now experts believe that there may be less than 30 left roaming free. It is feared that the wild South China tiger is likely to become extinct within the next decade. It is reputed to live in central and eastern China, with reports of tigers being observed in three isolated areas in south-central China — where small scattered populations are said to survive along the mountainous borders of Hunan, Jiangxi, and the Fujian provinces of south China. It has not been officially observed for over 20 years and the last unofficial sighting was a decade ago, but footprints and traces of droppings indicate that a few do survive.

Once it roamed through many of China's temperate upland forests, reveling in the dense jungle surroundings with abundant water for drinking and swimming in, but much of its habitat has now been destroyed. Poaching exacerbates the problem, especially as tigers have long been killed to provide ingredients for Chinese medicine. Traditionally, almost every part of the tiger served to cure one ailment or another. However, in 1993 China imposed a ban on traditional Chinese medicines made from tiger parts and has since sought foreign expertise and help with conservation and breeding to save this superb species. There are plans to locate and conserve China's tigers in protected areas in south central China in 19 reserves established within the tiger's supposed range, but viable populations of these fine predators do need vast areas in which to range freely.

There are also Siberian tigers *(Panthera tigris altaica)* in China but their numbers have also dropped dramatically.

Forest birds

Twelve threatened bird species breed in the subtropical forests of southeast China, including the dainty, brightly colored fairy pitta and the rare brown-chested jungle-flycatcher. The globally threatened silver oriole has a bold silver and black piebald plumage with a maroon-to-russet tail; it breeds in just a handful of reserves in Guangdong, Guangxi, and Sichuan, making a lovely fluting song as it takes to the air.

Many of these rare birds nest only in this subtropical forest region during the breeding season and migrate to other locations at other times of the year. Some, like the Reeves's pheasant *(Syrmaticus reevesii)* inhabit the forested mountainsides of central China where the trees tumble in a green wave over hills and lower mountain slopes. The wild population is declining, perhaps fewer than 2000 individuals still exist in what is left of the bird's original range, but this remains a familiar pheasant because it is bred in captivity in many parts of the world. It is named for naturalist John Reeves who sent the first specimens back to England in 1831.

China is the most important region in the world for the colorful pheasant family — it is host to 52 species out of a world total of 196. These most spectacular birds usually boast brilliant plumage with extravagant flourishes — elegant plumes, iridescent ocelli (eyespots) on their feathers, ear-tufts, ruffs, brightly colored facial skin, and inflatable pouches. Fine game birds include Chinese bamboo partridges, Elliot's pheasants, blue eared pheasant, Tibetan eared pheasant, Koklass pheasant, the elusive Cabot's tragopan — and the lovely silver pheasant *(Lophura nycthemera)* whose plumage ranges from dark gray through to brilliant snowy white finery. Usually silver pheasants lay eight eggs in a scrape on the ground beneath the cover of a bush and both parents help to rear the chicks. Brown eared pheasant *(Crossoptilon mantchuricum)* are poor fliers but fine gliders and good runners who will fight to defend a nesting territory. They live both in high mountain areas and the forest, building their nests in bushes or in small hollows on the ground — mainly in Shaanxi and Hebei provinces.

There are mustached laughing thrushes, and migrant blue-and-white flycatchers, handsome migratory songbirds that hunt from riverside bushes where the males flaunt their vivid blue plumage and enthusiastically trill their beautiful songs inbetween catching insects. The forests are also home to enormous Chinese blackbirds and the yellow-throated laughing thrush, which has a glorious deep blue forecrown that is in sharp contrast to its gaudy yellow throat and underparts. It flits between the ancient tall trees where it nests in groups. As dusk falls, black bitterns display busily. They breed in the reedbeds and build nests on reed platforms in shrubs or trees.

Small creatures must keep a wary eye out for the crested serpent eagle *(Spilornis cheela)* that haunts wooded areas near wetlands where it hunts mainly for snakes, lizards, frogs, and mice, after rising high on the morning thermals to scan the landscape with its keen eyes. Often it will perch on top of a tall tree before soaring off again over tree canopies. Pairs of eagles characteristically make a penetrating ringing 'kee kee ke' call to one another.

Other forest creatures

Tree frogs may be found in forests here, sometimes mating passionately in pools of water. The bright emerald Chinese gliding tree frog *(Polypedates dennysi)* is active at night in southern China and has huge appealing eyes that can see in the dark. All frogs enjoy the warm moist conditions in the forest, especially after a summer downpour.

The Chinese elephant *(Elephas maximus rubridens)* lived in the northeast but is believed to have become extinct by around the 14th century BC, a victim of hunting and habitat destruction. Today, a few Asian elephants *(Elephas maximus)* roam across southwest China. Wild Asian elephants used to migrate across the borders of China and Myanmar but have now settled down in a nature reserve in Yunnan province, China's sole habitat for wild elephants. Here small ones can be observed playing around in the paddy fields while the adults bathe in the river. The local people believe there can be no poverty or unhappiness in a place where elephants live, so they even tolerate the elephants eating their rice crops.

Left: The mossy green temperate forest floor in Jiuzhaigou.

Above left: A gloriously colored golden pheasant.

Above: Crested serpent eagles live in forests near fresh water.

Desert wilderness

China's Gobi desert is huge, ever-expanding, and justifiably famous but China's vast landscape has many other desert wonders to discover too. Some of the most important are described here to whet the desert appetite!

The Badain Jaran Desert in western Inner Mongolia covers 18,000sq miles (49,000km²) and boasts the tallest stationary sand dunes in the world, with some towering up to 1640ft (500m) high. Water flows underground here, formed by melted mountain snow that travels hundreds of miles through fractured rock. More than 100 spring-fed lakes lie between the dunes — some fresh, some highly saline — and these inspired the desert's name, which in Mongolian means 'mysterious lakes.'

Dzoosotoyn Elisen Desert is a remote, arid rugged area in the Xinjiang Uygur autonomous region: here lies the most land-locked point in the world (the most remote from any sea) at over 1615 miles (2600km) from the nearest coastline. It was reached in June 1986 by British explorers Nicholas Crane and Dr Richard Crane.

The Lop Desert (also in Xinjiang Uygur) is swept bare of sand by ferocious sand storms that blast across its terrain in a pall of dust to create monstrous dunes at the eastern end of the Takla Makan Desert. Wild camels gather to drink at the reedy oases on the northern desert edge.

The Ordos Desert is both desert and steppe in the south of Inner Mongolia. It is encircled by a great loop of the Huang River to the west, north, and east with mountains separating it from the Gobi Desert. In the south and east, the Great Wall of China separates the Ordos from more fertile lands. Here are sand dunes, rugged gorges, salt lakes, areas of montane grass, and shrublands. Wormwood grows here as well as the licorice root while forest thickets thrive along river margins and wild flowers flourish higher up the slopes. Rare birds breed in the saline lakes of the Ordos and, once upon a time, there were many wild two-humped Bactrian camels to be found here as well as snow leopards, Przewalski's gazelle, Przewalski's horses, and Asiatic wild asses. Today herds of goats and sheep predominate, cared for by nomadic Mongols who have lived here for centuries, often at war with the Chinese, but now peacefully raising goats as a source of cashmere wool.

The Takla Makan Desert ranks 15th in size in the globe's list of non-polar deserts and its vast sands cover an area of 104,250sq miles (270,000km²). It is around 621 miles (1000km) long and 250 miles (400km) wide and is whipped by frequent sand storms. It is crossed at both its northern and southern edges by branches of the famous Silk Road as merchants and travelers long ago sought to avoid this intimidating wasteland — there is absolutely no water to be found in the desert heartland. Merchant caravans would pause at oasis cities (many now in ruins) for respite.

Below: The Gobi Desert glows orange: this arid wilderness covers much of southern Mongolia.

Opposite: A well-preserved section of China's Great Wall. In some places the wall has been buried by desert.

Background: *Yaks graze on the sparse vegetation in the Mongolian desert. There are some 12 million yaks in the cold mountainous parts of China, comprising about 85 percent of the world's total population.*

Gobi Desert

This vast desert region stretches across China and southern Mongolia in the shadow of the mighty Himalayas that harvest the rain-carrying clouds and so deprive the Gobi of moisture. This is the fourth greatest desert of the globe — and Asia's largest. It occupies an arc of land some 1000 miles (1600km) long and 300 to 600 miles (480 to 960km) wide and covers an area of around 500,000sq miles (1,300,000km^2). It was part of the Mongol Empire and several important cities here flanked the Silk Road. Legends tell how the Gobi Desert was created when a Mongolian chief fled from the area with the Chinese army in hot pursuit. As he escaped, he used his black magic skills to dry up and shrivel the land behind him. Marco Polo and his father traveled across the Gobi Desert back in the 1200s and today the Gobi is still crisscrossed by caravans of nomadic Mongolian shepherds, cultured, hospitable survivors who have adapted to the rigors of living in the harsh desert conditions.

The Gobi is not predominantly sandy, but rocky. It remains a vast inhospitable expanse of barren gravel plains and rocky outcrops with a few drought-adapted shrubs, such as gray sparrow's saltwort and sagebrush, needle grass and bridlegrass. Temperatures can climb to 104°F (40°C) but may also drop to –40°F (–40°C) in winter, sometimes sprinkling the dunes with frost, or even snow.

The wildlife here includes wild asses and horses, rare Saiga antelopes, goitered gazelles, ibexes, marbled polecats, sand plovers, and the globe's last surviving wild Bactrian two-humped camels, one of the rarest and least studied of mammals. It is possible that 300 camels remain but this population is fast declining. Snow leopards and wolves stalk the ibex and other hooved animals. Some 30 Gobi bears (*Ursus arctos gobiensis*) live here too; these elusive creatures have longer limbs and a shorter golden coat than conventional brown bears to which they are related. This is the world's only desert bear but, when seen, it is generally in the Mongolian Gobi rather than the Chinese section.

This desert lures paleontologists and archeologists into its arid terrain as they search for dinosaur fossils in this veritable prehistoric graveyard, where many fossilized bones lie very close to the surface, especially in the northwest. The first fossilized dinosaur eggs to be discovered were found by an expedition party working in the Gobi.

The desert is expanding at an amazing rate. This vast area encompasses five distinct ecoregions: the Eastern Gobi desert

Background: *The arid Gobi desert landscape where in winter there may be snow on the dunes.*

Below: *Fossilized dinosaur bones at the Zigong Dinosaur Museum in Sichuan. The Gobi desert has many such buried fossil remains dating from Jurassic times, around 160 million years ago.*

steppe extends from the Inner Mongolian plateau in China north into Mongolia and includes the Yon mountains and many salt pans and small ponds; the Alashan Plateau semi-desert lies west and southwest of the Eastern Gobi desert steppe with many desert basins and low mountains; the Gobi Lakes Valley desert steppe, set north of the Alashan Plateau semi-desert; the Junggar Basin semi-desert; and the Takla Makan Desert (see also page 36). Dust storms whipped up by fierce winds sweep on across China.

Desert creatures

The terrain varies between shifting sand dunes where no vegetation survives, areas where less mobile sands are dotted with shrubs, and rocky, semi-desert areas with more stable soil where plants and shrubs can take root. The large Southern Altai Gobi reserve is home to one of two remaining populations of wild Bactrian camels. Przewalski's horses were last seen in the wild in this reserve — the only species of truly wild horse left in the world. They are similar to a domestic horse but smaller and more robust, with stripes on the back and shoulders.

China's desert mammals include a gerbil known as Cheng's jird (*Meriones chengi*) and small rodent-like jerboas that can burrow into the sand or race across it on long springy legs. Their hind legs are about five times the length of their forelegs while long flexible tails help them to maintain their balance as they leap an impressive 10ft (3m) in a single bound. Keen hearing and large eyes help them to steer clear of predators in the dark.

Reptile species include the Tartar sand boa, the frog-eyed gecko — a brilliantly colored nocturnal lizard endemic to Central Asia — and the Gobi gecko. Geckos are the most vocal of all the lizards, calling to others of their kind with chirping sounds and clicking cries. Their name derives from the Malay word *gekoq*, which sounds like their calls. Most geckos have no eyelids and instead sport transparent membranes over their eyes that need regular licking by the creature's long tongue to keep them clear.

Following pages: *Gobi Desert shrubs and grasses have adapted to survive drought and extremes of temperature that can often occur in the space of a day, as well as seasonally.*

The roof of the world

The Tibetan Plateau is often called the 'Roof of the World' and, with an average altitude of 16,400ft (5km), it is the highest and largest geological feature on earth. This vast plateau helps to funnel the latent power of Asia's great monsoons and acts like a towering reservoir, trapping and gathering huge volumes of moisture.

The highest mountain range in the world, the Himalayas, borders southwest China. Here many soaring peaks include Mount Everest (known as Mount Qomolangma in China). This is the highest mountain in the world at 29,035ft (8850m), topping the globe's greatest thrust of elevated peaks. As the two tectonic plates carrying Asia and India continue to grind into one another, Everest grows by an estimated 0.157in (4mm) a year. It is located on the border of Nepal and Tibet.

There have been more than 3000 ascents to the summit by over 2000 individuals, and nearly 200 people have died on the mountain. Following in their fathers' footsteps, the sons of Edmund Hillary and Sherpa Tenzing (who were the first to reach the summit in 1953) have also reached the peak.

Other major mountain ranges in China include the Changbai mountains on the North Korean border (their name means 'Forever White Mountains'); the rugged Tsinling mountains east of the Tibetan plateau that rise to 12,359ft (3767m) at Mount Taibai; and the Nan range in the south where peaks of over 6500ft (1981m) protect Guangxi autonomous region from the bitter Gobi winds — and once from unwelcome intruders like forces of the Han Empire.

China's Five Sacred Mountain Peaks

Pilgrims visit the Five Sacred Mountain Peaks here, which Han Emperor Wu Di declared sacred in the 2nd century BC: Tai Shan is the Taoist mountain of the east, in Shandong province, and is 5069ft (1545m) high with thousands of ancient carved steps, historic relics, and inscribed stone monuments. Heng Shan Bei, the spectacular mountain of the north, is set in Shanxi province and is 6617ft (2017m) high with a 1400-year-old hanging temple clinging to the edge of a precipice. Hua Shan, the mountain of the west in Shanxi rises to 6552ft (1997m) and is reached only by a steep perilous climb. Heng Shan Nan, the mountain of the south in Hunan province, reaches 4232ft (1290m) and is set in glorious scenery with magnificent Buddhist temples. Finally, Song Shan, the mountain of the center in Henan province,

summits at 4901ft (1494m) and is famous for its 72 temples on 72 slopes.

Other renowned peaks include Mount Lushan, towering high above the Chang River and Poyang Lake in Jiangxi province, ever swathed in mist; and the Jinggang Mountains in the border region between Jiangxi and Hunan provinces, famous as the starting point for Mao's Long March in 1934. Wudang Mountain in Hubei province has been an important Taoist center since the Ming Dynasty and is the site of many palaces and temples raised beside a winding mountain path that leads to the glittering Golden Hall. It was also the birthplace of the Wudang school of kung fu, the martial art.

Above: *The Tibetan Highlands — a symphony in copper, smoky gray, and icy white as desolate peaks rise some 13,000 to 15,000ft (4000 to 4570m) above sea level.*

Left: *Jade Dragon Snow Mountain in Lijiang, Yunnan, is the northern hemisphere's southernmost glacier, where 13 jagged peaks resemble the spine of an outstretched dragon.*

Left: The north face of Mount Everest: the ascent up the northeast ridge from Tibet is considered a tougher climb than the southeast ridge from Nepal.

Top: The snowy slopes of Everest glimmer in sunlight beyond Rongbuk monastery — the highest monastery in the world and situated near Everest's north-side base camp.

Above: Nyalam is perched on the brink of the Tibetan plateau at 13,000ft (4000m) altitude. A town of stone buildings, it is nicknamed 'The Gate of Hell' because the trail between Nyalam and the Nepalese border is considered so treacherous to negotiate.

Mountain forests and giant pandas

In southwest China, the landscape presents towering mountain peaks, steep valleys, and thick bamboo forests that lie shrouded by mist and cloud. This is the remote home of the giant panda, China's most celebrated wild animal. It is so rare and appealing that it was chosen as both the WWF emblem (WWF is the global conservation organization formerly known as the World Wildlife Fund) and as the logo of the China Wildlife Conservation Association (CWCA).

Today it is found in the wild only in the mountains of Sichuan, Gansu and Shanxi provinces at about 9850ft (3000m) above sea level. In the winter pandas sometimes make their way down to about 2625ft (800m) where it is warmer and more food is available. Figures vary, but some sources say only 500 wild pandas remain, while others claim 800 to 1000 survive. Following a comprehensive census and study published in 2004, WWF estimates that there are nearly 1600 pandas in the wild.

The giant panda (*Ailuropoda melanoleuca*) is an amazing creature that shares some characteristics with bears and some with raccoons and is classified as a bear subfamily. Some 4-5ft (1.2-1.5m) long and weighing 165-353lb (75-160kg), they have thick fur cloaking a white body and head plus black legs, ears, and eye patches that make them instantly recognizable. They shelter in any suitable cavity in trees or rocks, living on the ground but often climbing up trees to play, snooze in the sun, or to avoid a predator or bossy superior panda. They chew copious amounts of bamboo — a giant panda may eat up to 40lb (18kg) of bamboo a day. They also eat other plants, fruit, and small animals, such as bamboo rats.

Giant pandas are solitary animals and congregate with others only during the mating season. They are vulnerable because their precious habitat is vanishing (bamboo flowers only every 80 to 100 years and takes 20 years to reach a level that will sustain a panda group). Moreover, pandas have very few offspring and the young may be attacked by leopards. The Chinese government has set aside 12 panda nature reserves now where bamboo flourishes and bamboo 'corridors' allow them to migrate from one area to another.

Above: *Found only in China, the giant panda is one of the rarest animals in the world.*

Opposite: *One of China's lofty bamboo forests: pandas need to eat up to 40lb (18kg) of bamboo each day to survive.*

Opposite: A giant panda must eat bamboo shoots for some 12 hours a day to obtain enough nourishment from this tough, nutritionally poor food source.

Background: The scarcity of bamboo forests greatly limits the range of pandas. Moreover, great sweeps of bamboo die after they flower — which occurs after a lifespan of around 80 years.

Mountain fauna and flora

The southern slope of the Qin Mountains in Qinling Shan in north China is the last spot in the world where the crested ibis (*Nipponia nippon*), one of the rarest birds in the world, survives in the wild. It has been hunted almost to extinction for its long white breeding plumes and was thought to have vanished by the 1960s until just seven were discovered in China's Shanxi province in 1981. Usually it lives in the trees, coming down to the ground only to hunt; it likes to be near wetlands where it can find fish, frogs, crabs, and insects.

China's mountains are also home to the snow leopard (*Panthera uncia*). This is the most beautiful of Asian wild cats with soft, spotted gray and black fur that provides good camouflage in the stony landscape. It leaps nimbly across the rocks at an altitude of 6600 to 20,000ft (2000-6000m) and hunts blue sheep on the Tibetan plateau and in Xinjiang, Gansu, and Inner Mongolia. It is now protected as it is so rare and elusive. There are also brown bears, wolves, ibexes, and wild mountain sheep called Gobi argali (*Ovis ammon*) — the males sport two large corkscrew horns.

Golden monkeys live in forests (see also page 32) but also often scurry about in rhododendron thickets in the high mountains of central and western China in Yunnan, Guizhou, and Sichuan provinces. These high areas are snowbound in the winter but the monkeys' sturdy bodies are covered with long thick fur, particularly over their shoulders, and this protects them from the winter cold when they can survive by eating lichens. They live at altitudes of 5900 to 9850ft (1800 to 3000m).

Other rare and endangered species here include the Sichuan jumping mouse, a katydid (a large grasshopper-like insect) which has been seen only once since it was described in 1933, and the giant Asian hornet, which is around 2in (50mm) long with a wingspan of about 3in (76mm). Local villagers call it the 'Yak Killer' because of its deadly potent sting, which is strong enough to kill a human.

Secretive and gentle red pandas (*Ailurus fulgens*) live in forested mountain slopes in the southern Chinese Himalayas where their name means 'small bear-cat.' They seek refuge in rock dens and old hollow trees or spend the day drooped

Above: Sometimes called 'grunting ox,' yaks can climb to altitudes as high as 20,000ft (6000m).

Opposite: Red pandas with their white snouts blend in well among the forest's russet moss and white lichen.

over a high tree branch or sleeping curled up with tails wrapped around heads. They generally awake at dawn and dusk to feed, running swiftly along the ground or through the trees. Like their black and white cousins, they eat mainly bamboo but sometimes nibble berries and fruit, fungi, roots, acorns, lichens and grasses, eggs and fledgling birds, or small rodents and insects. They drink by placing a paw into water and then licking up the liquid. The first known written record of the red panda occurs in an ancient Zhou dynasty scroll, while Major General Thomas Hardwicke was the first European to describe a red panda in 1821, 48 years before giant pandas were similarly described.

There are approximately 12 million yaks (*Bos grunniens*) in China. They live mostly in cold mountainous areas in remote areas of the Tibetan plateau and adjacent highlands in Gansu province where they graze on the alpine grasslands in the summer and on any shrubs they can discover in the deep winter snow when their long coarse hair and dense woolen undercoats insulate them remarkably effectively against the freezing temperatures.

Fifteen species of the beautiful blue poppy flaunt their gorgeous petals in the Himalayas, seeming to reflect the azure skies and icy blues that are such a characteristic feature of Yunnan and Tibet. They are sometimes used in traditional medicine and grow best beside cool streams where their delicate flowers seem to glow in the evening light. Magnolias open their gorgeous rosy flower cups in the Himalayas while countless slipper orchids flourish in the Sichuan mountains and wild rhododendrons carpet the southwest China slopes with their spectacular blooms.

Left: *Over 2800 tree species grow in China's forests, which are hosts to amazing animals such as giant pandas, golden monkeys, and Reeves's pheasants. China has an amazing range of landscapes including bamboo forests, tropical jungle, mountains, glaciers, coral reefs, and deserts. It also encompasses Earth's highest and one of its lowest points. This great diversity of habitats hosts over 12 percent of the world's plant and animal species.*

Below left: *The delicate pale mauve blossom of a rhododendron: these flourish in mountainous zones including the Chinese Himalayas. Other gorgeous flowers originating in China include the azalea, camellia, gardenia, hibiscus, chrysanthemum, and tree peony — China's national favorite.*

Above: *Slipper orchids can survive icy conditions under a blanket of snow and then bloom once this melts. Many rare orchids flourish in highly specific habitats: the golden slipper orchid of Yunnan* (Paphiopedilum armeniacum) *grows on just one range of limestone hills and cliffs.*

Background: At UNESCO (United Nations Educational, Scientific and Cultural Organization) World Heritage Site, Mount Huangshan, or Yellow Mountain, the elements converge — Earth rises in high peaks, crags, and rock columns to meet swirling clouds and mist.

Opposite inset: In Yunnan's Stone Forest, an amazing panorama of karst limestone peaks and high pillars — sharpened by wind and rain erosion — thrust their serrated edges skyward.

Earth — the element

Considering the vast sweep of subject matter that discovering China's landscape encompasses, a single chapter can scarcely begin to do justice to the wonderful variety of terrain that the Chinese 'Earth' can assume and the myriad creatures that live here, and the people who make their homes in hill, mountain, plain or plateau, woodland or jungle. This chapter is just a brief taste of this overwhelmingly vast, impressive, and often stunningly beautiful place.

In Chinese medicine and cosmology, the element Earth has associations with millet or rice, cattle, dates, the yellow phoenix; it has to do with the mouth, the sense of taste and sweet things. It is also associated with land and mountains, wind, and singing. It is the center of things and so seems an ideal place to begin our journey, to seek the essence of China, its central core — for the landscape is the foundation upon which all else rises.

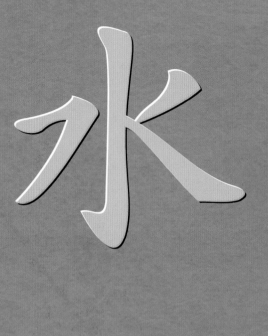

水

WATER

China is a huge nation — it has a mighty landscape, and endless plains and high mountains that rear up inland in the west. A vast proportion of its huge area butts up against the land mass of many other Asian territories and the soaring Himalayas. However, China's eastern and southeastern fringes are coastal, lapped by three seas — from north to south the Yellow Sea, the East China Sea, and the South China Sea, all of which form part of the mighty Pacific, marking the ocean's eastern perimeters.

Left: *Night falls over China's Yangshuo peaks, turning both river and sky a deep magical blue.*

Mariners' tales

Many a sailor returned to Europe with tales of Oriental riches and bustling ports — no doubt sometimes embellished in the afterglow of memory but nonetheless painting a vivid picture of the lure of the East and the very special flavor of the Chinese world. For so long for Europeans China was a secret land, until Venetian trader and explorer Marco Polo found fame as one of the first Westerners to travel the Silk Road in the latter part of the 13th century. In due course, he was received at court by the Great Mongol ruler Kublai Khan (grandson of Genghis Khan) and ultimately trade relations with this vast realm were established. Today China's shores are dotted with many ports, with Hong Kong perhaps the most renowned of these vibrant coastal hotspots.

The Yellow Sea

This great gulf is a semi-enclosed body of water that washes the eastern Chinese mainland and, on its western fringes, the Korean Peninsula. It measures some 620 miles (1000km) long from north to south and is 435 miles (700km) wide from west to east, with many small islands clustering near the Korean coast. Here the Huang (Yellow River) and Chang (Yangtze River) ooze yellow mud that is deposited in the shallow waters, turning it the color that accounts for the sea's name. The inlet of Korea Bay forms part of the northeastern Yellow Sea, squeezed between China's Liaodong Peninsula and western North Korea. In 1904, this sea was the scene of a mighty naval battle off the Shandong (Shantung) Peninsula during the war between Russia and Japan.

This is one of the largest shallow areas of continental shelf in the world with sea depths only reaching 230 to 260ft (70 to 80m). It is a major overwintering ground for both fish and invertebrates and is edged by vast mudflats that are home to countless waders and flocks of winter visitors; some two million birds may be in transit during the migration season. The water's surface temperature can change dramatically and, despite some warm currents, the sea turns cold and rough during the monsoon season. In winter, some sections become bleak ice fields.

Right: Hong Kong at night, seen from Jiulong. Hong Kong has the world's greatest skyline, comprising at least 7681 skyscrapers, placing it ahead of anywhere else in the world, despite the fact that New York is larger in area.

Life in the sea

The strange-looking dugong enjoys feeding on seagrass in the warmer waters here but it is now vulnerable to extinction on a global scale. Meanwhile, sea cucumbers or trepang scavenge the debris on the sea floor but they are themselves

regarded as a culinary delicacy by the Chinese. Mighty gray whales journey through these waters as do many turtles, including the leatherback, the world's largest turtle that dives deep in search of food such as jellyfish. Loggerhead turtles consume jellyfish too, seemingly immune to the powerful toxins of Portuguese men o' war. They can stay submerged for up to seven hours at a time, emerging at the surface for only a few minutes before diving down again. Other turtles include the green variety that nest on China's southern beaches and hawksbills, named for their beak-like mouths.

Left: A green sea turtle swims in open water. About 50 days after green sea turtles have laid their eggs by night on sandy beaches, the hatchlings emerge and rush to the sea.

Below: A serene landscape in a Chang River gorge. The waters have risen since the building began of the new Three Gorges Dam in 1994.

Bottom: Chinese text on a sea boulder, Hainan Island, China.

The Chang River empties into this busy stretch of water, which is full of islands and submerged reefs in its northern parts. It covers an area of 482,280sq miles (1,249,000km²) and is connected to the South China Sea by the shallow Taiwan Strait. It merges with the Yellow Sea in the northwest. The most significant port here is scintillating Shanghai, China's largest city. Originally a fishing town, it developed into China's most important city during the early 20th century (see the *Cities* section on page 210). The East China Sea that washes its shores drops to an average depth of 1200ft (350m). Here fishing hauls may include cuttlefish, tuna, and cutlass fish.

South China Sea and islands

After the five oceans, this sea is the world's largest body of marine water, covering some 1,351,500sq miles (3,500,000km²). It is traversed by a vital shipping sealane — a veritable maritime superhighway and an important element in Asia's industrial revolution. Called the Southern Sea by the Chinese, its waters stretch between Singapore and the Strait of Malacca in the southwest up to the Strait of Taiwan in the northeast. It has rich natural resources, such as oil and gas, but is subject to multiple international disputes over territory and resources, as well as smaller-scale problems,

atolls, shoals, sandbars — and over 200 small islands.

Discovered by the Chinese during the Qin Dynasty (221–207 BC), the South China Sea islands have been variously called the Tough Heads of the Surging Sea, Coral Cays, the Thousand-Mile Long Sands and the Myriad-Mile Stony Embankment. Although home to only a few indigenous people now, some of the houses here date back to the Tang or Song Dynasties that stretched between the 7th and 13th centuries AD. Long ago, Hainan fishermen recorded the time needed for sailing between the different islands, and described some 200 sea routes and the fishermen's names for over 100 islands. Famous Chinese mariner Zheng He (see page 73) voyaged past the islands in the 15th century and an atoll in the Spratly Islands is named for him. During the early 20th century the Republic of China claimed the islands as part of Canton province and later they fell under the Hainan administrative region.

Below: Shanghai's skyline dominated by the Oriental Pearl Tower, Asia's tallest and the world's third highest tower.

Opposite: Rocks loom before a distant view of Hong Kong — this shining metropolis was once just a small fishing village beside the turquoise South China Sea.

Left: China's eastern and southeastern shores meet the Yellow Sea, East China Sea, and South China Sea. There are countless islands in these waters.

Top: The gleaming silver tuna found in China's seas are fast, agile swimmers, able to cut through the water at speeds of up to 43mph (70kph).

Above: There are cuttlefish in the East China Sea as well as many species of fish including yellow croakers, mackerel, Chinese herrings, jellyfish, shrimps, and crabs.

Hong Kong and Macau area

First incorporated as part of Imperial China during the Qin Dynasty, Hong Kong Island, which lies just off the Jiulong Peninsula, originally served as a center for fishing and farming, then became a trading post and naval base during the time of the Tang and Song Dynasties. It was occupied by the Portuguese from 1557 and then flourished as a British crown colony from 1842 until 1997. Today this beautiful port and island is a major financial center and home to what has been described as 'the most thrilling city on the planet' (see also page 222).

There are many islands in this region with Lantau being the largest in the territory. The coast hereabouts follows a tortuous, indented route, emerald waters wrapping around many a promontory and crinkly-edged island. Traditional stilt houses cluster on the muddy banks while junks, sampans, and fishing vessels busy themselves about the contorted shoreline.

During June's annual dragon festival and regatta, great crowds of spectators applaud as ornately carved and painted vessels race to honour Qu Yuan (c.340-278 BC), a faithful servant of a long-gone Chinese emperor and one of China's first great poets. Everyone eats a local delicacy called *zongzi* — glutinous rice balls wrapped in bamboo leaves.

Above: Containers are unloaded in Victoria Harbour, set between Hong Kong Island and the Jiulong Peninsula.

Right: The unforgettable view of Hong Kong at night, as the highway sweeps toward glittering skyscrapers.

Following pages: Thirty-seven miles (60km) southwest of Hong Kong, this elegant Macau bridge connects the two islands.

Whales in Chinese waters

Whales may be seen in the waters off China but they are becoming increasingly rare. In the western Pacific, the barnacle-encrusted gray whale *(Eschrichtius robustus)* swims along in the ocean between eastern Russia and southern China's shallow coastal waters. The western population of this superb creature, which is believed to have winter calving grounds in the South China Sea, is critically endangered; only about 120 of these 30-ton giants are thought to remain in this region.

Short-finned pilot whales *(Globicephala macrorhynchus)* may occasionally be spotted in the South China Sea; they have distinctive bulbous foreheads and sometimes seem to swim together in a sort of 'chorus-line' — in pods that may number several hundred individuals, hunting for fish and juicy squid.

Boats and voyages

Chinese archeologists now believe that the nation's history of boat-building may date back some 7500 years for they have unearthed a wooden boat (the most ancient vessel ever discovered in China) near Xiaoshan City in Zhejiang province. It is a dugout canoe with two wooden pegs shaped like tree stumps on each side. Several oars and some timbers have been found at the site where experts believe that, long ago, people used to build boats by the river. Neolithic relics such as pottery, stoneware, and jade articles — some dating back 8000 years — have also been discovered here.

Junks developed during the Han Dynasty (206 BC–AD 220) and evolved into one of the most successful ship designs. Some historians think that these sturdy ships crossed the oceans as early as the 3rd century AD. Long afterward their sail and hull designs would inspire Western shipbuilders. Flags were hung from the masts to bring good luck and one legend tells how the clouds above the ocean hid a dragon that, when angered, blew up typhoons and storms … but as he liked bright flags (especially red ones) with Chinese writing on them, these were often flown by mariners to be on the safe side!

The largest junks were built to withstand the rigors of global exploration and 15th-century medieval travelers in Asia described huge vessels of about 2000 tons, some 400ft

(120m) long. The largest ever built were probably those of Admiral Zheng He (also known as Cheng Ho), famous for his seven voyages undertaken six centuries ago in fleets of 200–300 ships carrying over 28,000 men. Some information in the ancient Chinese chronicles is now disputed by modern scholars but he certainly seems to have sailed to many nations, visiting southeast Asia, India, the Middle East (including Egypt), and Africa. Some claim that he even circumnavigated the globe and reached the American continent 70 years before Christopher Columbus! His fleet of junks incorporated treasure ships that boasted space for a crew of 1000, with the flagship under the commander's charge, as well as horse ships carrying tribute goods and repair essentials, supply ships with food for the crew, water tankers, warships, and patrol boats.

Opposite: Victoria Harbour: sturdy Chinese junks like this may have sailed the oceans since around AD 200.

Above: William Alexander's 1796 engraving of Tchin-Shan (Golden Island) in the Yang-Tse-Kiang (Great River of China).

Right: A Chinese junk sails into Hong Kong harbor.

A land of many rivers

China abounds in rivers and, like everything else in this nation of superlatives, the rivers are big! Most of them cover huge distances and more than 1500 drain areas of 386sq miles (1000km²) or more. The Qinghai-Tibet plateau is the source of most of the major rivers that descend from great heights from their sources in the mountains to reach the plains and, eventually, their estuaries. This means that China is very rich in hydropower potential but today there are fears of possible over-exploitation of this resource.

The Chang, Huang, Heilong Jiang, Zhu, Liaohe, Haihe, and Huaihe rivers flow to the east and empty into the Pacific Ocean. The Yarlung Tsangpo River in Tibet first flows eastward and then ripples south into the Indian Ocean. The Ertix River reaches northward from the Xinjiang Uygur autonomous region up to the freezing Arctic Ocean. Meanwhile, stretching over 1354 miles (2179km), the Tarim in southern Xinjiang Uygur is China's longest interior river, while countless others flow on until they reach inland lakes or disappear into salt marshes or deserts.

The Chang River

The Chang (or Yangtze) River in central China is, at 3915 miles (6300km) long, China's largest river and the third longest in the world, after the Nile and the Amazon. The lands that border the middle and lower Chang River benefit from a warm and humid climate, plentiful rainfall and fertile soil, making these vital agricultural regions. The deltas of

both the Chang and Huang (Yellow) rivers help to create fertile arable land. The river serves as an important transport route, too — often called the golden waterway, the Chang links west and east, with its deep natural channels encouraging navigation and making it a veritable transportation artery.

In its higher reaches, however, its course makes many sharp turns, and it plunges through narrow passages and gorges, including the famous and spectacular scenery of the sheer Three Gorges (Qutang, Wuxia, and Xiling). This part of China has been threatened for some years by the raising of the greatest hydroelectric river dam in the world that spans some 7660ft (2335m) across the Chang. Rising 607ft (185m) high, the Three Gorges Dam is expected to be fully operational by 2011 and its ecological impact has been the subject of much heated debate. The extremely rare Chinese River dolphin has probably vanished already. In recent years, only a few individuals have been recorded as remaining in the wild and in 2007 it was declared extinct by scientists.

The river still supports an impressive array of biological wealth, however, including countless migratory birds and a largely endemic population of 400 fish species, including the Chinese sturgeon. The Central Chang is a globally important ecoregion as well as being economically significant — with all the potential threats that brings — so a difficult balancing act must be maintained here if the wildlife is to survive. Not only will wetlands be greatly affected by the dam but, ultimately, so will people too — over five and a half million individuals who live in the surrounding area will lose their homes or be encouraged to relocate.

Background: A coppery sunrise at Yangshuo — where the gleaming Yulong and Li Rivers reflect the spectacular limestone pillars and peaks.

Below: The silver ribbon of the Chang River loops lazily around a conical peak.

Left: *When fully operational, the Three Gorges Dam hydroelectric power station will be the world's largest, with 34 generators supplying a total capacity of 22,500 megawatts.*

Below: *Some species of fish in the Chang River are on the brink of extinction so now fishing is periodically banned to allow dwindling stocks to recover. Here a solitary boat slides across the rippling waters.*

Opposite: *Sheer cliffs rise abruptly to tower over the Yangtze River. Vegetation clings tenaciously to the craggy surfaces of the 2-million-year-old Qutang, Wuxia, and Xiling gorges.*

Rare cranes and alligators

The bogs and marshes here are a vital winter refuge for some 95 percent of the world population of critically endangered Siberian white cranes *(Grus leucogeranus)*. These birds display with their heads thrown back and beaks pointing skyward, and variously flapping wings, dancing, bowing, running, jumping, hurling sticks and grass about, and making a complex pattern of co-ordinated calls.

Mainly found in the middle and lower reaches of the Chang River, the Chinese or Yangtze alligator *(Alligator sinensis)* is one of the world's rarest crocodilians. During the past several decades, the population has decreased dramatically and it is now highly endangered. The 3000 surviving in the 1960s have now been reduced to an estimated 140 or so in the wild. In a rescue operation, their eggs are now being hatched at a Chinese alligator reproduction center in Anhui province and some 10,000 Chinese alligators have emerged in captivity through these artificial means. These alligators use their long sharp teeth to crush the shells of snails and mussels. They also eat fish, frogs, and rats but, unlike their American relatives, rarely attack large animals. They live in groups of two to 11 reptiles and dig elaborate dens in which they hibernate. They also create 'gator holes' that fill up with water, helping many other water creatures to survive times of drought.

The Huang River

The Huang (or Yellow) River in the north-central area is China's second largest, with a length of 3395 miles (5464km) and the world's sixth longest. It is bounded by lush pasturelands and areas rich in mineral deposits. The river rises in the Kunlun Mountains in northwestern Qinghai province and then courses through nine provinces and autonomous regions as over 30 tributaries and countless streams feed its flow on its way to the Bohai Sea delta. Near Zhengzhou in Henan province, the river slices through the Loess plateau, where erosion has taken place forming a long continuous gorge. Wonderful natural scenery is

complemented by a rich history and cultural heritage for while the ocher-yellow waters of this great river irrigate many farmlands and carry a heavy load of silt, the area is as famous for enriching minds as it is for fertilizing lands.

The river valley is called the cradle of Chinese civilization, the spiritual home of the Chinese people. Known as the Mother River by the Chinese people, this was where many Neolithic, Bronze, and Iron Age sites flourished and, since those early cultural beginnings, the river has continually inspired authors, poets, and artists — as well as giving rise to many legends. Legendary heroes from this time include Suiren-shi who taught the Chinese to make fire by drilling wood and Fu His, the first of China's mythical emperors, who devised how to hunt, trap, fish, and write. Shennong-shi invented agriculture. Thus, in this prosperous region, the scene was set in both history and fable for many emperors to lead ancient China's civilization onward to amazing levels of learning and accomplishment.

On the downside, the river running in full spate across the flat northern plains can cause devastating floods,

Above: *China's second biggest waterfall — the magnificent yellow Hukou Falls in the Huang River's middle reaches.*

Opposite: *Critically endangered Chinese alligators stay cool in slow-moving rivers, streams, lakes, and swamps.*

especially when the cascading water bursts its banks — an event that has occurred more than 1500 times in the last 2500 years, altering the river's main course about 18 times and gradually moving it farther south. Many people have been drowned, while survivors have had to endure dire famine and disease. In 1887 there were an estimated 900,000–2,000,000 deaths and in 1931 up to 4,000,000 may have perished. Today a series of dams and flood protection measures guard against the repetition of such tragedies. Sometimes flooding is not caused by natural events. During the Second Sino-Japanese War, in 1938, Nationalist troops deliberately broke the dikes and let the river overwhelm 33,554sq miles (54,000km²) of land; as many as 900,000 people may have died.

Above: At Hukou Falls, the yellow-tinged waters surge forward to the pounding cascade.

Opposite: In severe winter weather, the Huang River freezes, as here at Pianguan Pass, where the Great Wall of China meets the bank of this mighty watercourse.

The Zhu River

The Zhu (or Pearl) River courses its way through the south of China for a distance of 1375 miles (2214km). Once its delta was a quiet farming area but today this is the scene of dynamic development. It is often called 'the world's workshop' on account of the millions of electronic gadgets, watches, clocks, toys, books, clothes, and textiles that are manufactured in this region. Unperturbed by all this change, the river flows on into the South China Sea emerging between Hong Kong and Macau.

Back in 1657, European explorer Peter Mundy voyaged along the Zhu River and reported that 'the Porpoises here are white as Milke, some of them Ruddy withall.' What he had actually seen was the rare Chinese white dolphin (*Sousa chinensis chinensis*). This is a subspecies of the humpback dolphin — the population along the Chinese coast is unique because their skins are colored pink. Scattered groups of them often haunt shores close to Hong Kong and when the new airport was built, a campaign was launched to highlight their plight. A grinning cartoon dolphin served as the mascot for Hong Kong's return to China in 1997. Measures were taken to reduce the loss of habitat impact caused by land reclamation and now about a thousand survive in the Zhu River — one of the world's highest populations. Newborn dolphins are gray but become soft pink in color as they mature. Locals claim that the dolphins near Hong Kong are the world's rosiest.

Mekong, Yarlung Tsangpo, and Amur Rivers

The Mekong River (otherwise known as Mother of All the Waters, the Nine Dragons River, the River of Rocks, and the Great River) flows from its source in China's Qinghai province near the border with Tibet, traveling southeast to the South China Sea, crossing Yunnan province. It stretches around 2700 miles (4350km) by the time it reaches the sea in the south of Vietnam near Saigon (Ho Chi Minh City), with some half of its length being in China. Its upper reaches are full of steep descents and swift rapids.

The Yarlung Tsangpo River rises at the Jima Yangzong glacier near Mount Kailash in the northern Himalayas in southwestern Tibet, where it flows across southern Tibet, traveling east for about 1000 miles (1700km or so) at an average altitude of 13,125ft (4000m). It is the highest major river in the world. The river forces its passage through the mighty Himalayas by means of several great gorges and then,

as it reaches its easternmost point, makes a massive loop around Mount Namcha Barwa where it forms the Yarlung Tsangpo Canyon in Tibet. This is claimed to be the deepest and largest canyon in the world, some 314 miles (505km) long and 19,715ft (6009m) deep at its deepest. It plunges from an altitude of some 9840ft to a mere 984ft (3000m to 300m) at the end of the gorge. Today this is a popular, if extremely challenging, place to kayak and is nicknamed 'Everest of Rivers.' The river flows on southwest and then south through India and Bangladesh, becoming known as the Brahmaputra in these countries.

The Amur (or Heilong) River stretches from west to east, flowing though northeast Asia and is, in fact, formed by the convergence of two rivers — the Shilka, which has its source in the eastern slopes of Mongolia's Khentii mountains and the Argun that is born on the western slopes of the Great Khingan range in China. These two tributaries join forces in Heilongjiang province, China, to become the Amur proper. This forms a 1000-mile (1600km) long natural boundary between eastern Russia and northeastern China. The river is about 2700 miles (4340km) long in total of which some 1925 miles (3100km) flow through China. It is the largest undammed river in the world.

Above: *Rivers and streams thread their contorted passage through the bronze Mongolian plains. Many of these run into salt lakes or disappear into the arid rocky Gobi soil, but some course on underground, allowing fresh water to be tapped by means of wells.*

Left: *An evening sunset paints both the sky and the Yarlung Tsangpo River the color of molten gold as a fisherman tends his nets. This is the world's highest major river, averaging an altitude of 13,125ft (4000m) in Tibet.*

Following pages: *Clouds scud above the Yarlung Tsangpo River in Tibet. From its source in the northern Himalayas, the river flows east first — for about 1056 miles (1700km) — before descending south into Arunachal Pradesh in India.*

globe. It was built section by section in different areas and dynasties and was then joined together during the Sui Dynasty (581-618), greatly strengthening both economic and cultural links between north and south China as it

by nine rivers over which 104 bridges have been built.

Opposite: Boats line a narrow canal that courses through a southern Chinese town.

Spectacular waterfalls

The tumultuous Huangguoshu Waterfalls (or Yellow-Fruit Tree Falls), sited southwest of Anshun city in Guizhou province, are the best known of a cluster of some 18 falls and are China's (and Asia's) largest with their steepest drop descending some 243ft (74m) and with an impressive width of 266ft (81m). The three main cascades are called the Waterfalls Cluster, Water-Curtain Cave, and Rhinoceros Pool (Xi Niu Tan) named for its rotund curves. At the Silver-Chain Waterfall, linked cascades mingle to tumble downward in a tumult of white spray.

Hukou (or Kettle Spout Falls) is the largest and most magnificent yellow waterfall in the world, set in the middle reaches of the Huang River in Yichuan county, Shaanxi province. The water tumbles down 100ft (30m) into a deep riverbed in a turbulent, thundering rush of foam, bubbles, and spray. Mist rises as the river seems to smoke and countless rainbows flirt with the sunshine, creating translucent arches and vibrant flashing ribbons of color.

Other large waterfalls include Changbai Waterfall, a 223ft (68m) cascade in the Changbai peaks in northeast China bordering North Korea. This puts on its most powerful display when the mountain snows melt. It is the highest volcanic waterfall in the world. Detian Falls in the hills of Guangxi province mark the Vietnamese border and served as one of the crossing points for the Chinese forces during the Sino-Vietnamese War. Close by is the Tongling Gorge with its own unique plantlife and cliffside caves where local bandits once hid both themselves and their treasure. The 131ft (40m) wide Diaoshuilou Pubu Falls at the northern end of Lake Jingpo in Heilongjiang province are impressive when fed by the summer rains and equally so in winter when their more delicate cascades freeze into an ice curtain.

The Pearl Shoal Waterfall in Jiuzhaigou, set high in western Sichuan province, is a beautiful crescent-shaped tumble of water that plunges some 1300ft (400m) and is 533ft (162m) wide. The Yarlung Tsangpo River boasts three major waterfalls, the largest of which is called the Hidden Falls — it was not recorded in the West until 1998 when it was discovered by a party of kayakers exploring the Yarlung Tsangpo Canyon.

Opposite: A broad gushing curtain of water tumbles over Pearl Shoal Waterfall in the Jiuzhaigou Valley.

Below: Visitors admire the plummeting Huangguoshu Waterfalls.

China's lakes

China has over 104,460sq miles (270,550km²) of inland lakes and waterways, most of which lie on the middle to lower Yangtze plain and on the Qinghai-Tibet plateau. There are freshwater lakes such as Taihu and Hongze and the two largest — Dongting and Poyang — in the central Chang. Set to the north of Jiangxi province the vast expanse of Poyang Lake encompasses 1383sq miles (3583km²). It is the largest freshwater lake in China. Saltwater lakes include Nam Co and Siling Co and huge Qinghai Lake (the Blue Lake) in northeast Qinghai province, which covers 2200sq miles (5694km²). This is one of the country's highest inland saltwater lakes, and is home to abundant fish and vast flocks of birds that perch on its islands. It is the largest mountain lake without a river outlet in central Asia.

The vast floodplains along the Chang provide habitats for about 300 species of bird that include endangered migrants like cranes and storks, as well as 200 fish, over 84 mammal, 60 amphibian, and 87 reptile species. The nature reserve of Dalaihu (Hulun Nor) spreads over 1545sq miles (4000km²) and includes a brackish lake, which is China's fourth largest. Here marshes and reed beds provide a good breeding habitat for Japanese cranes, great-crested grebes, Oriental white storks, and relict gulls.

Unfortunately, some 50 years of intensive land reclamation, together with the widespread raising of dams, dikes, and polders, have encouraged agriculture and urban settlements to spread across former flood plains and lakes with inevitable habitat fragmentation that threatens the future of many endangered species.

Heaven Pool is a two-million-year-old volcanic crater lake at the summit of Mount Changbai on the Sino-Korean border and is the largest volcanic crater lake in China at 3.80sq miles (9.82km²). It is found at an altitude of 7054ft (2150m) and is completely cut off in winter. China's largest nature reserve in one of her few areas of dense forest is found here. It serves as a habitat for the exceptionally rare and massive Manchurian (or Siberian) tiger, of which fewer than 20 survive in China.

Kanas Lake in Xinjiang Uygur was formed 200,000 years ago and is China's deepest freshwater lake, dropping to 604ft (184m) at one point. Nearly 800 plant and 117 bird species flourish in these surroundings. The Siberian taiga forest extends into the Kanas region supporting a range of subarctic wildlife. Over 1400 Tuvan people live in the region too, descendants of ancestors that arrived here from Siberia over 1000 years ago to become cattle-breeding nomads, tending herds of goats, sheep, camels, reindeer, and yaks and living in their traditional yurts, covered by felt or bark or hide teepees.

Today Kanas Lake is famous for its superb color palette, varying — as it mirrors the changing weather and skies — from turquoise blue to green, deep blue, slate gray or sunset pink. Legend has it that this lake is home to a group of gray, smooth, seal-like finned creatures — not unlike Scotland's solitary Loch Ness Monster. Apparently, these creatures swim in parallel pairs, whipping the water into white bubbles and leaving a wake of ripples behind.

Mention must also be made of West Lake, at the center of Hangzhou city in east China, which is known for its elegant bridges, pavilions, and calm surrounding hills. Over the centuries, it has inspired many poets and artists: poet Su Shi compared its soft allure to Xi Shi, one of the Four Beauties of ancient China.

Left: *West Lake, Hangzhou, where the water shimmers and the mountains are shrouded in a veil of mist; this was a favorite imperial retreat.*

Opposite: *Tibet's Namtso Lake — in 2005 named as one of China's five most beautiful lakes. It is the highest altitude saltwater lake in the world and its water is crystal-clear blue.*

Left: *The reflective quality of water is one of its most beautiful characteristics. Here pagoda tiers are highlighted in a pink glow that also shimmers in the reflections in the water below.*

Background: *Great expanses of plain and water stretch across the Mongolian landscape under vast skies. In this remote region there are often spectacular sunsets in glorious shades of orange and pink.*

Wetland wildlife

Many cranes strut and preen in China's wetlands. The world is home to only 15 species of crane, of which China has eight. These elegant birds have often inspired paintings, music, poetry, dance, embroidery, and sculpture. The crane symbolizes longevity, good fortune, and dignity but it is threatened today by pollution, excessive hunting, and loss of habitats so the Chinese government has now established several natural reserves to help protect these beautiful birds.

The red-crowned crane (*Grus japonensis*) is the second rarest crane in the world and is known as a symbol of luck, dignity, and fidelity. The estimated wild population is less than 2000 individuals. It stands 55in (140cm) tall and can fly great distances but then settles in the reedy marshlands to feed on fish, worms, and frogs. When spring comes, many breed in the middle and lower reaches of the Nen Jiang River in marshlands that form part of the Zhalong Nature Reserve. In winter, birds stalk the lakes and marshes of the Chang River's lower reaches.

Rare black-faced spoonbills (*Platalea minor*) stand about 3ft (1m) tall. Deep Bay in Hong Kong serves as one of their main winter haunts — numbers here have risen in recent years. The estimated global population is still only around 1000 but this is a marked improvement on the estimate of 288 made in the late 1980s.

One frog in China warbles and flutes with such versatility that its high-pitched calls resemble those of birds, primates, or even whales for their range and complexity. This is the Chinese concave-eared torrent frog (*Amolops tormotus*). It has an extraordinarily rich and complex vocal repertoire, with multiple upward and downward sweeps of notes and amazing ultrasonic frequencies — all produced by two pairs of vocal sacs.

The giant water salamander (*Andrias davidianus*) lives in clear unpolluted streams and rivers at altitudes of 3200 to 8200ft (1000 to 2500m) above sea level. It is the globe's largest salamander, capable of growing up to 6ft (1.8m) long, though most are considerably smaller. Their rough dark skin is porous to assist with respiration as they lack gills. Their tiny lidless eyes are set atop a broad flat head.

The beautiful water arum blooms in the high marshes and bogs of China's northeast at altitudes of up to 3600ft (1100m). Their yellow flowers cling to a spadix, encircled by a gleaming white, petal-like spathe. They are sometimes called water dragons.

Below: A family of red-crowned cranes search for fish, oblivious to their status as the world's second rarest crane.

Opposite: Water arums thrive in China's wetland marshes.

Left: Water lilies, common throughout China, belong to the Nymphaea *genus*, derived from the Greek word for female water or tree spirits.

Above: Chinese cuisine uses lotus seeds and roots while the flowers are considered to be emblems of purity, fruitfulness, and creativity.

Below: *20-million-year-old carp fossils have been discovered in China as well as the first written mention of koi, which are a type of ornamental carp prized for their wonderful colors. Goldfish have been kept here as ornamental pond fish for centuries.*

Water — the element

In the Chinese interpretation of the elements, water represents solitude, privacy, introspection, philosophy, mystery, truth, honesty, anxiety, nervousness, and insecurity. It is an important part of both Chinese philosophy and Chinese topography. Chinese gardens usually feature a central pond and several streams, the softness of water contrasting with the solidity of the rocks while the pool surface reflects the constantly changing sky above. Carp and goldfish may be part of an aquatic scheme that aims to soothe the mind, aided by the therapeutic sound of a waterfall.

A literal translation of feng shui is 'wind water' and it is believed in China that indoor fountains and water features also play a vital part in the home. Flowing water is seen as an embodiment of positive energy and, correctly placed, is believed to bring abundance and wealth into the home or workplace. Of all the elements, water is the one mostly associated with wealth. This is scarcely surprising as water is the giver and preserver of life, the original source of all the living things that thrive on the planet today.

Above: Water sparkles like jade in Black Dragon Pool Park in Lijiang where there are waterfalls, swaying trees, and bridges.

Left: A pool with golden carp, waterfall, ferns, and rocks creates this garden's miniature landscape.

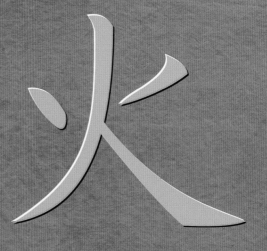

In Chinese astrology, fire is one of the basic elements and forms of energy — all the five elements are described as being in a constant state of change, affecting and flowing one into another throughout the natural world. Fire is fundamental to all of us — it keeps us warm and allows us to cook and control of it epitomizes the intelligent state — man is assumed to have become fully human once he made tools and lit fires! It has been an important part of our culture and religious practices ever since.

Left: *To the Chinese, red symbolizes fire and the south and is associated with weddings as well as virtues such as courage, loyalty, fortune, fertility, passion, and happiness.*

The meaning of fire

In China fire is associated with the planet Mars, the color red, and warmth. In Chinese astrology fire denotes strength, dynamism, persistence, restlessness, and excitement. Those people born in the years of the fire are expected to be strong leaders, good at self-expression, decisive, and positive; they are warm people who love adventure and innovation. Fire is also believed to govern the heart. Moreover, and most importantly for the contents of this chapter, fire ignites inspiration and imagination and the practical application of this: human creativity.

Creativity and culture

Creativity refers to everything that is made — an all-encompassing sweep of how people express themselves. Consequently this chapter concentrates on the human state, and on our skills and pleasures, whether expressed through culture and celebration, art, religion, or simply flying a kite!

China's culture has developed throughout its long history, finding many different modes of expression over six millennia. As one of the earliest centers of human civilization, it boasts the longest continuously used system of written language on the globe. Traditionally the very first dynasty was that of Xia (2033–1562 BC) and early Bronze Age discoveries in Henan province would seem to support this. By the time of the second, the Shang Dynasty (1562–1066 BC), there is clear evidence of settlement along the Huang River in eastern China. History has started to accumulate and in 221 BC the Qin Dynasty took power — in this period the role of the Emperor and a standardized Chinese language would be established.

Chinese culture encompasses a vast spectrum of art forms and styles, all infused with the special quality of the East, whether the expressive form is painting, sculpture, music, dance, opera, or circus.

Of course, architecture also plays a major role in the development of how a nation expresses itself. This subject will be explored in the final chapter of this book (Metal), so suffice to say here that cities, buildings, homes, gardens and the shape of how we live are always important elements in cultural development and that China's architects have evolved many incredible forms of edifice. These range from exquisite ornate pagodas to the dramatic shapes of the skyscrapers that stud many skylines today, especially those of Hong Kong and Shanghai.

Above: For more than 4000 years, Chinese calligraphy has developed as a refined art form and means of communication. Even the order in which the strokes of the characters are created is considered to be of great importance.

Opposite: The serene face of an ancient Buddha sculpture. It was the explorer Marco Polo who first brought back to Europe reports of the magnificent art and architecture in China.

Above: *Longhua Temple in Shanghai has a fine fountain and wonderful Song-period seven-story pagoda with bronze bells hanging from each corner of its eaves.*

Right: *In Beijing's Forbidden City are found many carved dragons, phoenix — and lions. The king of the animal kingdom, the lion denotes august power.*

Chinese art

The Neolithic period was marked by pottery and jade and the Shang Dynasty (1562–1066 BC) by bronze casting embellished with fine detail. Each dynasty that followed was greatly influenced by the major thinkers and teachers of the time. Bronze is especially associated with Chinese culture and this material was used by sculptors to create many masterpieces including animal-shaped drinking vessels. The first primitive porcelain entered the arena around AD 600 and eventually the creation of this material became such a highly refined process that the word china was used in Britain to imply beautiful porcelain (see also page 126).

From the 4th to the 8th century, Buddhist art flourished. Calligraphy and painting rose to the fore in the royal courts, with much fine work executed on silk, even after paper was invented. As the Sui and Tang Dynasties progressed between AD 581 and 907, Buddhist architecture and sculpture thrived, influenced by Gupta-period Indian art, while the Song Dynasty (AD 960-1279) inspired evocative landscape paintings with soft blurred outlines and mountain contours potently suggesting distance.

Through the Ming Dynasty (1368–1644) both painting and printing discovered a wider color range and simplicity gave way to more detailed styles of composition. During the late Qing Dynasty (1644–1911), traditional Chinese art peaked and then began to mutate as it absorbed outside influences. Today Chinese art explores modern techniques but is often still influenced by traditional techniques that honor the ancient masters. Gradually, as Western influences and techniques penetrated, a new form of realism emerged as Chinese artists became fully international.

Opposite: The stylized female figures in this ancient Chinese fresco are executed in subtle browns and blues. Fresco painting demands speed and simplicity as the pigments quickly soak into the plaster on which they are delineated.

Below: In traditional Chinese architecture, every facet of a building was decorated. Here, brilliant blue and turquoise tones, with pink and white floral motifs, embellish circles, segments, and curves on the painted wooden ceiling of an ancient pavilion in Beijing.

Music and entertainment

Early music in China made much use of percussion instruments until string and reed instruments emerged. The first Chinese operas developed during the Song Dynasty near present-day Shanghai but it was the Qing Dynasty (1644–1911) that witnessed the emergence of the renowned Beijing opera in the 18th century. This is one of the best-known forms of Chinese opera, which presents a brilliantly colorful mixture of music, mime, speech, dance, singing, acrobatics, and combat skills. Cantonese opera emerged later.

Much traditional Chinese dance has a military basis — once upon a time dancers held weapons and moved as a coordinated group. This evolved into military-style exercises but then later dance became symbolic of beauty and joy and absorbed local folk dances. Today, China's contemporary styles of dance and ballet seek a new expression but they are often founded upon traditional dance, Chinese opera, and the martial art of kung fu.

Puppetry and shadow theater are revered art forms in China. Shadow plays first appeared in the Han Dynasty as a means to cheer up Emperor Wu (who ruled 141 BC to 87 BC) after the demise of a favorite concubine. Her form was made of leather and its shadow cast by an oil lamp appeared to come to life. During the 13th century, shadow performances entertained the Mongolian troops while they were resting from duty in their barracks and it thus spread to Arabia, Persia, and Turkey as the Mongols made military conquests. Then the stories were often Buddhist tales or depicted heroic warfare feats. Now, however, shadow plays generally enact traditional fairy tales and myths. The puppet head is always removed at night — and often stored separately — to avoid any risk of the puppets coming to life under cover of darkness!

Entertainment in China often involves clowns and acrobats. Records of the Chinese circus date back over 2000 years to the Qin Dynasty (221–207 BC) but it undoubtedly began long before that and may have developed from local folk art or from imperial court entertainers — or both! Some 250 circus troupes perform within China today and often tour abroad, with the Chinese State Circus being the most famous. Acrobats perform amazing feats, balancing, tumbling, and dancing while the traditional Chinese lion, a symbol of good luck, has been dancing for thousands of years, its origins dating back to the early Qin and Han Dynasties. It is not confined to the circus; both lions and dragons feature in New Year's parades, at the consecration of temples, in religious rites, at planting and harvest festivals, at the opening of important buildings or the launch of a new business — in fact, at just about any celebration.

Left: Chinese acrobatics began around the 4th century BC as a popular, highly skilled entertainment for ordinary people.

Opposite: A Beijing opera performer with stylized make-up and an elaborate and colorful costume and headdress.

Left: A Beijing opera singer must undergo a long apprenticeship to master the many skills required, first learning acrobatics, then singing and gestures. Some students will become musicians rather than performers. In earlier times, all female (Dan) roles were played by men.

Here be dragons

Dragons matter here! Sometimes special parades feature immense paper models. Dragon kites are flown at celebrations, dragon-shaped boats race one another, and countless legends celebrate these powerful fire-breathing beasts. A typical Chinese dragon is a writhing scaly composite of deer horns, camel head, devil eyes, snake-like neck, large cockle-shaped belly, carp scales, eagle claws, tiger paws, and oxen ears.

In contrast to its Western counterpart, a dragon is a power for good, rather than evil. It wards off wandering evil spirits, brings prosperity and good fortune and signifies greatness, goodness, and blessings. Wise, but sometimes vain, it is believed to be a ruler of weather and moving water — waterfalls, rivers, or seas — and may appear as a waterspout or tornado. It can divide and divert floods but, if angered, may be destructive, calling up floods or drought. Sometimes it coils up in the land to form mountains.

The first legendary Emperor Huang Di (b. 2704 BC) was said to have been immortalized as a dragon and, as the

Above: A long snake-like dragon with four claws. Chinese 'dragon bones' were often sold as traditional medicines but these were probably dinosaur fossils.

Opposite: This close-up view of a dragon carving in the Imperial Palace, Beijing, exhibits overlapping scales, curling whiskers, sharp fangs, and heavy brooding brows.

Chinese consider him their ancestor, they sometimes call themselves the 'descendants of the dragon.' The Chinese dragon has been a symbol of imperial power ever since Huang Di's time, especially yellow or golden ones with five claws on each foot. Emperors were supposed to bear dragon-shaped birthmarks; their throne was called the Dragon Throne and people believed that emperors could change themselves into these creatures whose carved depictions feature on so many flights of steps, royal palaces, and tombs. A dragon appears on the national flag of the last Qing Dynasty (1644–1911).

Many cities have pagodas where people traditionally burned incense and prayed to dragons. Such is the respect that this fiery beast has always commanded, that the disfiguring or inappropriate use of a dragon image still causes an outcry in China today. The Year of the Dragon, which takes place every 12 years, is considered especially lucky and children born then are expected to enjoy health, wealth, and a long life.

Dragon legends may initially have been inspired by fish, snakes, or perhaps crocodiles, for these reptiles are said to sense the onset of rain. Stories tell how dragons are able to transform themselves into water, clouds, or fire. They can fly and hide among clouds or under water; they disguise themselves as silkworms; they swell to the size of the universe; they become invisible or glow in the dark.

Such stories have long been part of an oral tradition, with one generation passing on these amazing tales by word of mouth to the next, but dragons have also proved an exciting subject for artists to depict in paintings, on fabric and in many other media. In carving, there are nine principal ways to represent them: set atop bells and gongs because dragons call loudly when attacked; on the screws (tuning pegs) of stringed instruments as dragons love music; on the tops of stone tablets for they love literature, too; at the base of stone monuments where they support the heavy weight; on temple eaves where they are ever alert to danger; on bridge beams since dragons like water; on Buddha's throne where they like to rest; on the hilts of swords as these mighty beasts can kill; and, lastly, carved on prison gates for some dragons are quarrelsome trouble-makers.

Dragons feature in many poems and books too, while it was the yellow dragon that supposedly introduced the first of the mythical Three Sovereigns, the legendary Emperor Fu Xi (mid-2800s BC) to the elements of writing.

Writing and calligraphy

Early Chinese poetry was greatly influenced by Confucius (551–479 BC), Qu Yuan (c. 340–278 BC), a renowned Chinese poet and thinker, and the earliest known collection of Chinese poems called the *Book of Songs*. Lyric poetry called *Ci* expressed feelings of desire and rose to the fore in the Song Dynasty. Some of the earliest recorded writings were court archives, while classic Chinese works include *I Ching (Book of Transformations or Changes)*, a system of cosmology and philosophy written nearly 3000 years ago to guide those seeking the true balance of the universe's natural elements. The paired opposites of Yin and Yang were central to this historic divinatory guide that remains part of Confucian and Taoist philosophy.

While literature became widespread with the invention of printing (see page 120), calligraphy remained a vital medium. Calligraphy means 'good writing' but, however pleasing to the eye, there is far more to it than that. It is the medium through which language becomes art, an abstract but sublime form of expression with a history dating back over 4000 years. Calligraphers were (and are) highly respected and during the Imperial era, good calligraphy skills were essential for anyone aspiring to be a court executive.

Tu Meng of the Tang Dynasty (AD 618-907) developed 120 expressions to describe different calligraphic criteria and styles — seal, official or clerical, regular, running or semi-cursive, cursive, and so on. Each one has its own characteristics and purpose. While there are some 32 brush strokes in all, there are only seven main ones (known as the Seven Mysteries). The choice of paper and its thickness and quality of absorption, the brush style and flexibility, and controlling the concentration of ink allows the artist to create an infinite variety of styles and forms. Every character is regarded as a beautiful flower.

Previous pages: *Brilliantly colored ceramic tiles on the Nine Dragon Wall (built 1756) depict nine dragons playing with jewelry balls. Beijing's two dragon walls are in Beihai Park and the Forbidden City.*

Below and opposite: *Traditional Chinese calligraphy characters emerged from Han Dynasty clerical script.*

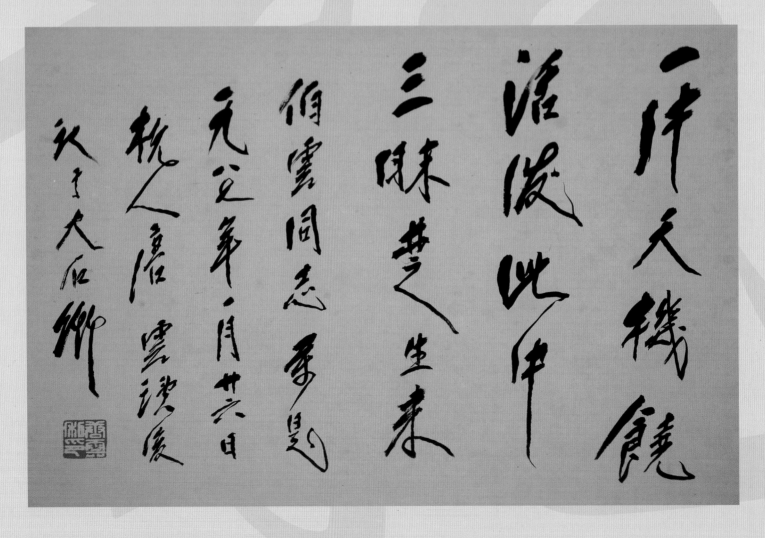

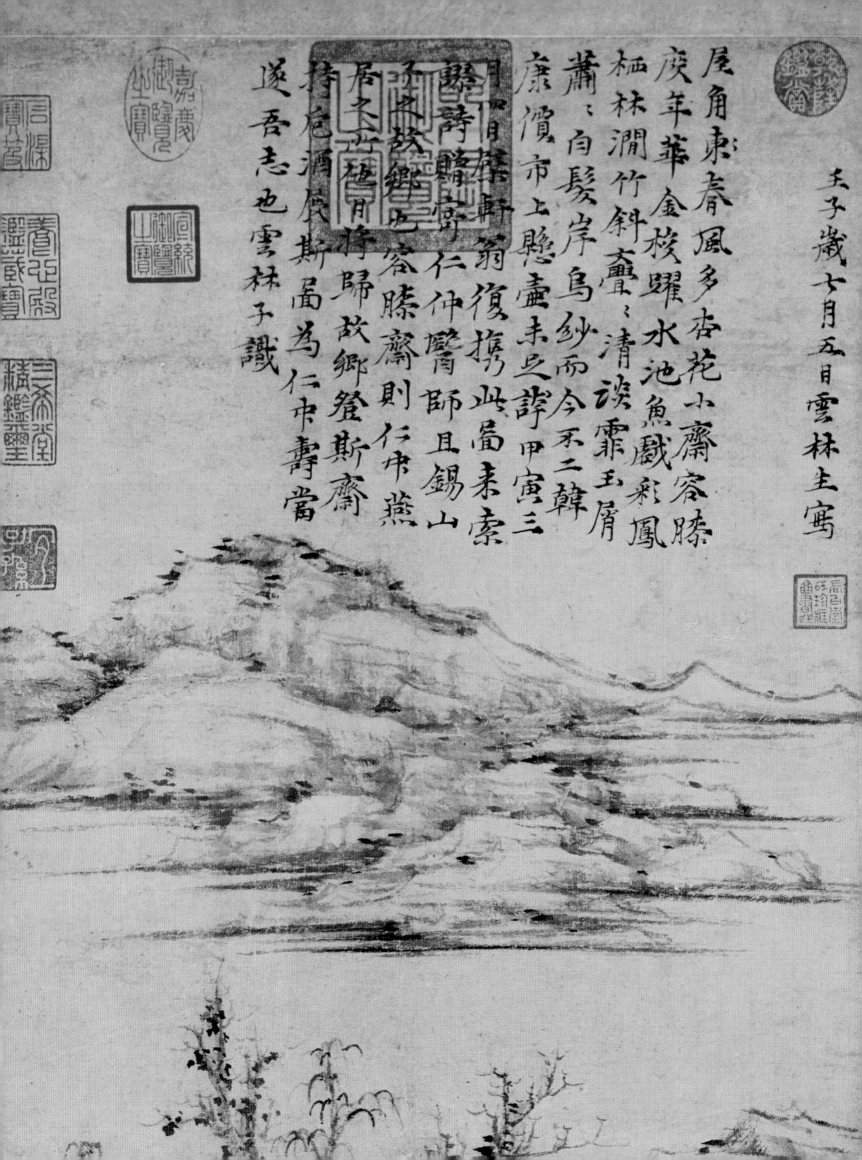

壬子歲七月五日雲林生寫

屋角東春風多杏花小齋容膝
庾年華金梭躍水池魚戲彩鳳
栖林澗竹斜奪清談霏玉屑
蕭蕭白髮岸烏紗而今禾二韓
康濱市上懸盧未必誇甲寅三
月十日簡軒翁復攜此冊素索
縣詩贈寫仁仲醫師且錫山
頑石故鄉容膝齋則仁仲燕
居之所又將持歸故鄉登斯齋
持尼洒辰斯冊為仁仲壽當
遂吾志也雲林子識

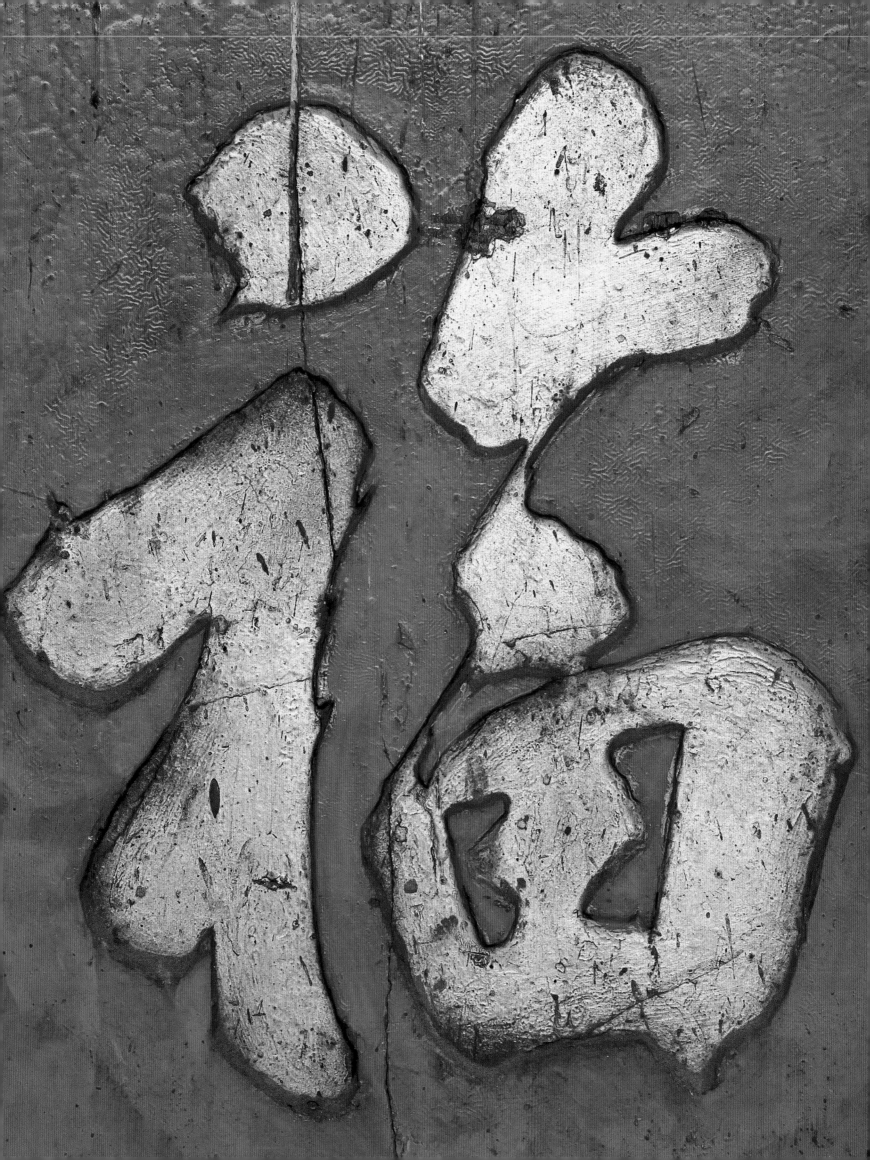

Ink, paper, and printing

If China is renowned for spearheading the art of handwriting, it is also famous as the place where ink and printing developed. The Chinese invented and perfected what is now ironically named Indian ink. Some historians think that the Chinese may have discovered ink up to 5000 years ago, but its first recorded invention was by philosopher Tien-Lcheu in 2697 BC. By 1200 BC, ink was in common use in China.

Chinese ink was first made from the soot of pine smoke or burning vegetable oils, which were thickened with a glue made from gelatin derived from donkey skin and the musk of young deer. This early ink was used to blacken the surfaces of raised stone-carved hieroglyphics. Sold in solid ink sticks or ink cakes, often shaped like a canoe, the ink was ground on an inkstone and mixed with water. It did not fade but was difficult to make and very rare and expensive until the 10th century, when lamp oil soot was used.

The Chinese brush was said to have been invented by Ming Ti'en in the 3rd century BC. Often paintings were executed on silk while heavy, rather clumsy books were made of bamboo. Some 2000 years ago, in AD 105, a Chinese official at the Imperial Court, Ts'ai Lun, invented the process of making paper by grinding plant fibers into a pulp, then drying and forming this into thin sheets. He used the waste from silk production or mulberry tree bark and other plant fibers as his raw materials. Papermaking remained a great secret until about AD 700 when knowledge of it spread to Japan and then was brought to Spain by Arabs who had captured some Chinese papermakers.

Printing is considered one of ancient China's four great inventions (the other three are the compass, gunpowder, and paper). For over 3000 years, wood, bone, horn, stone, and metal seals were used to disseminate information. Decrees, texts, scriptures, poems, and images were inscribed on wood, bronze, or stone and then copied by rubbing the engraved images onto paper. Later individual sheets were pressed against woodblocks carved with text and illustrations; these were being used in the Tang Dynasty (AD 618-907) but patterns had been printed on cloth centuries before. By 1023, the central government was using copperplate printing to create another Chinese invention — paper money!

Previous pages: Calligraphy inspired other forms of artwork, including seal carving, inkstones, and beautiful paperweights. Here it decorates ancient wooden doors.

Opposite: This sturdy old printing block was a means of duplicating a Tibetan Buddhist scripture.

Right: This Chinese banknote uses printed calligraphy. Paper currency emerged locally in China in the 600s, spread widely during the Yuan Dynasty but was 'put on hold' (along with trade with the Western world) in the 15th century. Early banknotes were printed on paper made from mulberry bark.

Below: Ancient Yi (a minority religion) scriptures on fragile-looking paper.

More Chinese inventions

China was the land in which many new concepts took root. Advances in knowledge were made in mathematics, the prevention and diagnosis of illness and the four technologies said to have had the most dramatic impact on the world — as mentioned previously, these were printing, papermaking, navigation using the compass, and gunpowder.

Printing and papermaking allowed knowledge and information to be readily spread and shared and provided universal access to education. Of course Gutenberg's printing press accelerated this process in Europe in the 1400s but without the ink and the paper to print upon, this would not have happened.

Originally devised for divination and to determine the most propitious alignment of buildings, the compass developed to play a vital role in advancing the accuracy and security of navigation on land and sea. With regard to seafaring, the Chinese also devised the rudder, hull compartments, paddle wheels, dry docks, and mobile (rather than fixed) sails.

Gunpowder had a dramatic impact on excavation and construction technology as well as its more obvious uses in warfare. It is thought that gunpowder was discovered in the 9th century AD by Chinese alchemists searching for an elixir of immortality. The crossbow also originated here, as did firearms, rockets, grenades, and landmines.

Imagination and inspiration

The imaginative Chinese also discovered the circulation of blood in the human body, the mathematical concept of zero, and how to cast iron. They devised planting and hoeing techniques, the seed drill and the iron plow, while the awe-inspiring list of Chinese inventions also includes the technology to drill for natural gas, mechanical clocks, fishing reels, church bells, harnesses and stirrups, wallpaper, and umbrellas to protect from both rain and sun. They hung suspension bridges on bamboo cables and built rainbow bridges that arched over waterways without needing the central pillars for support that were so vulnerable to China's fierce floods.

The first seismograph, credited to Zhang Heng (AD 78–139), Royal Astronomer in the late Han Dynasty, was a cast bronze vessel containing a pendulum and decorated with nine dragons facing in different directions and with nine frogs sitting below. Seismic activity made a particular ball fall from one dragon's mouth to a frog's jaw and thus indicated the direction of the tremor.

The secret of silk

The Chinese knew how to make silk by as early as 1300 BC and were trading it with the Roman Empire and Byzantium by the 2nd century BC. Roman women adored wearing Chinese silk; this valuable commodity reached the West overland via the route named for it — the Silk Road. For years Europeans tried to discover how to make this wonderful fabric but did not unravel the secret until about AD 550, when monks brought back silkworm eggs from China.

Above: The Chinese have been making explosive firecrackers for over 1000 years, originally with bamboo casings to hold the gunpowder and later in paper containers.

Opposite: Fireworks, believed to ward off evil spirits, get the New Year off to a brilliant and ear-splitting start.

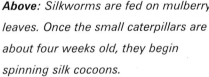

Above: Silkworms are fed on mulberry leaves. Once the small caterpillars are about four weeks old, they begin spinning silk cocoons.

Opposite: Beautiful embroidered Chinese silk — this luxurious fabric was trafficked along the Silk Road and led to trade with Europe.

Left: The magnetic compass developed from the lodestones (that align north-south) used in China to tell fortunes.

The creative power of fire

Fire has many uses — it helps to clear ground, to warm people, to deter dangerous predatory animals, to cleanse and purify objects, to melt and mix metals, to make tools, weapons, cooking utensils — and to cook the meals that sustain us. Many Chinese delicacies are now enjoyed in the West, but in China food has long been seen as both nourishment and medicinal therapy. Cuisine specialists served the emperor at the Imperial court and during the Tang Dynasty (AD 618-907) food therapy became very popular; many classic books were written on the subject.

Beautiful, white, delicate porcelain has to be fired at an extremely high temperature to reach its final perfection. Also called china after its place of origin, fine clay pottery was made first during the late Eastern Han Dynasty (AD 25-220) after potters of the early Yin and Shang Dynasties began using kaolin, a rare white clay. The first piece of true porcelain was probably not produced until the Tang Dynasty while the finest porcelain skills would not be fully mastered and exploited until the Ming Dynasty (1368-1644).

Italian explorer Marco Polo brought back porcelain to Europe from China in 1260 and, in due course, this fine china was exported throughout the world and was much admired wherever it appeared. At one time, especially in medieval Europe, antique porcelain was interchangeable with gold and jewels as a symbol of wealth. Many spies were sent to China to attempt to discover how it was created until the secret of the extra mineral ingredients needed was at long last discovered by Europeans — some 450 years after they first saw it — when Johannes Friedrich Böttger identified the correct formula and the need for very hot kilns in 1709.

The 1790 blue-and-white design of the willow pattern plate made in England by Josiah Spode was inspired by a Chinese pattern called Mandarin. It depicted a Chinese boat, a bridge with people upon it, a temple, two birds in the sky, and a willow tree.

Above: Chinese cuisine and cooking pots have developed over 5000 years.

Right: A blue and white 'kraak' dish of the 1600s. Until 1709 only the Chinese knew how to make porcelain.

Beauty in the sky

Kites were invented in China more than 2000 years ago during the warring states period (475-221 BC). They copied the shapes of butterflies and birds, and the first examples were made of wood. Some were able to stay in the air for several days and so are sometimes regarded as the earliest form of aircraft. Initially kites were used for military signaling and communication, testing the direction and strength of the wind, and measuring distances. It is recorded that large kites were sometimes used to lift warriors up into the air to observe enemy movements or to fire down on them with bows and arrows, while other kites were used to scatter propaganda leaflets or to send an urgent message requesting help or back-up or carry exploding fireworks to scare an opposing army.

Background and opposite: Celebrations add warmth and color to life — with Chinese kites being part of the fun. Developed from military surveillance, despatch and communication tools, kite-flying became part of popular culture and a competitive sport.

During the Tang Dynasty (AD 618-907), people began to use kites for rather more recreational purposes, such as hanging from them bamboo strips that vibrated and sang in the breeze. During the later Qing Dynasty (1644-1911) it was considered that letting a kite go (or picking up a lost one) might bring bad luck. Today the kite is celebrated in many festivals in China.

Some are national celebrations, others local or ethnic festivals. As well as kites, bright lights, lanterns, decorations and flowers augment these colorful occasions throughout the Chinese year.

Kites and competitions feature in many celebrations. The Weifang Kite Festival, held each April in the city of Weifang in Shandong province, is one of the world's largest, an exciting event that attracts hundreds of participants and some 60,000 or so spectators who watch an astounding variety of kites fly. Many designs have a symbolic meaning in folklore or history: tortoises, cranes, and peaches signify long life; bats mean good luck; butterflies and flowers denote harmony; a dragon means power and prosperity. Kites with soft wings may depict insects, goldfish, clouds, flocks of swallows, or even octopuses. These competitions are followed by a superb hour-long firework display. In Tianjin's 1983 competition (Tianjin is a municipality about 60 miles [100km] southeast of Beijing that is one of China's major kite-making centers), a 100-section, 328ft (100m) kite, shaped like a dragon-headed centipede, was flown by a squad of six skilled men.

Spring Festival

The Spring Festival is when families gather to celebrate in homes that have been given a special spring clean ready to welcome in the Chinese New Year while the crowded city streets blaze with lanterns. Flower-decorated red lanterns hang outside houses, stores, and office buildings, while calligraphic inscriptions and New Year paintings bedeck front doors. Families enjoy a sumptuous dinner; some stay up all night. There are lion dances, dragon lantern dances, land-boat races, stilt-walking, carnivals, and parades. In south China people eat *nian gao*, a New Year cake, while in north China, they enjoy jiaozi dumplings shaped like crescent moons. Firecrackers explode in rural areas while the skies above cities and towns glitter with spectacular firework displays. Parents and grandparents give children lucky

Above: *Chinese dumplings include jiaozi eaten at the Spring Festival when they are usually shaped like crescent moons.*

Opposite: *The lion dance is part of Chinese New Year celebrations. The calligraphy (inset) denotes Spring.*

money in special red envelopes and on the first day of the New Year, everyone wears new clothes as they wish each other good luck and happiness.

Beautiful multi-colored lanterns are strung everywhere during the Lantern Festival that is celebrated on the first full-moon night in the Chinese New Year with fireworks and guessing lantern riddles — a tradition that began in the Song Dynasty (AD 960–1279) when people wrote special riddles on lanterns. *Yuanxiao*, stuffed rice dumplings in soup, are eaten to symbolize staying together.

Ancestors and dragons

At the traditional Qingming festival (which normally falls in April), people commemorate their lost ancestors, tidying up family graves and placing before them offerings of wine, food, and fruits. They then burn *zhiqian* (paper made to resemble money), smarten up the graves with fresh soil and branches, and then enjoy a picnic.

Summer's traditional dragon boat festival (which falls either in May or June) can trace its origins back over 2000 years and commemorates the poet Qu Yuan. People row boats out onto their local river, throwing pieces of rice-stuffed bamboo into the water as an offering to this patriotic poet, who drowned himself in the Miluo River in 278 BC when in despair at the decline of his nation. Today the festival is marked by daughters returning home, the hanging up of Zhong kui's portrait (he was a legendary ghost-catcher who drove away demons) beside the doors of home, temple, and office to keep out evil spirits, welcoming the ghost boat and martial art competitions. Calamus and Chinese mugwort are hung up to ward off illness, realgar or calamus wine is drunk, and special dishes eaten including wudu pie, salted eggs, fresh vegetables, and *zongzi* (also called *jiaoshu* or *tongshu*) — leaf-wrapped pyramids of sticky rice with many variations including ham, pork, and beans.

In August the traditional mid-fall festival at the time of the full moon remembers how the emperor of Qi met Wuyan, a young woman who was supposed to be ugly but whom the emperor saw as beautiful in the moonlight. He fell in love and made her his queen. The moon is also supposed to house the beautiful goddess Chang'e whom young girls wish to emulate. In ancient times, people would offer elaborate cakes as sacrifices to the moon goddess and so the tradition of eating moon cake developed as a symbol of family unity and togetherness.

Top: At Chinese New Year, children are given lucky coins securely wrapped in bright red envelopes.

Above: Ghost money (or joss paper) is burned in earthenware pots or special chimneys during ancestor worship.

Left: Glowing red lanterns celebrate Chinese New Year.

Right: *An illuminated float at the dragon boat festival when dragon-shaped boats race. Standing an egg on end just as noon strikes is said to bring good luck for the next year.*

Below: *A street parade graced by beautifully costumed stiltwalkers celebrates Chinese New Year.*

Right: *At the mid-fall festival, Chinese tea is drunk and people enjoy eating moon cakes, a special delicacy often filled with lotus seed paste.*

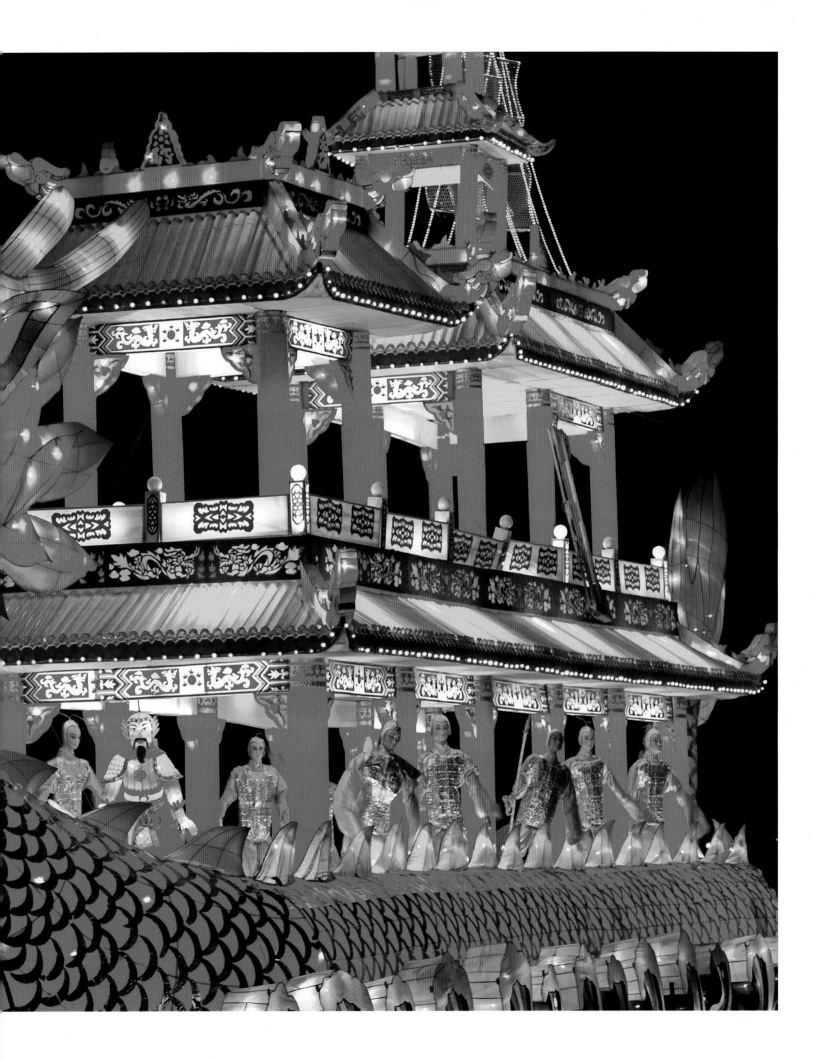

Double Seven and Double Nine

Ever since the Han Dynasty, Qi Xi or the Double Seven Festival is celebrated on the seventh day of the seventh lunar month. Rather like Valentine's Day, it celebrates love and remembers how an honest orphan fell in love with the seventh daughter of the Emperor of Heaven. They married in secret but the Emperor missed his daughter's expert weaving of clouds and rainbows and sent her grandmother down to fetch her back. The grandmother made the Milky Way in the sky to separate the pair but magpies, sympathetic to the broken-hearted couple, flew up to Heaven to form a bridge for the pair to meet once a year on the evening of Qi Xi.

The Double Ninth or Height Ascending Festival is held on the ninth day of the ninth lunar month. This is the time to ascend a high hill, eat tower-like cakes composed of nine layers, drink wine, and admire chrysanthemums. It has now mutated into a festival to honor older people who are invited to the celebrations and associated theatrical performances by younger friends and relatives.

Ice and snow festivals are held in Harbin in northwest China from December to March every year and they date back to Manchu times (1644–1911). Today they feature hundreds of the most amazing and elaborate ice and snow sculptures, some of which are vast — there may be ice temples, bridges, and even a Great Wall ice slide. Ice lantern tours and suitably wintery sporting events take place in the city where temperatures can drop to −36°F (−38°C).

Above and right: Magnificent ice sculptures at the Harbin Ice and Snow Festival, the largest and most extravagant event of this kind — but one now threatened by global warming.

Religion and philosophy

Throughout the centuries the Chinese people have explored their potential through the way they think — philosophy, intellectual argument, religion and ideology, science, and medicine. They have made the most of themselves and their surroundings through disciplines such as feng shui and the martial arts. Meanwhile their creative energy is expressed through literature, the arts, music, and many ceremonies — when tea may be drunk as a sign of respect or to express gratitude or an apology.

The number of temples dotted around the landscape is an indication of the variety of religions followed in this vast nation. They include Taoism, Confucianism, Heaven worship, Islam, and a scattering of Christianity and Judaism. Buddhism is the largest organized religion in China; it took hold during the Han Dynasty and, supported by many emperors, follows the teachings of the prince from Nepal who gave up his wealth to seek enlightenment. It involves self-discipline, a belief in the oneness of everything, and the practice of meditation. Today some sources estimate that Buddhism, in one form or another, may be followed by as many as 1 billion Chinese, making it the country with the largest number of Buddhist followers in the world.

The emergence of Zen (Chán) as a distinct form of Buddhism was first recorded in China in the 7th century AD. Followers of Zen Buddhism believe they should look inside themselves for enlightenment and understanding of the nature of Buddha, rather than searching outside themselves for answers. This search within is known by several terms, such as 'introspection' or 'turning the eye inward.'

Above: *A cluster of burning incense sticks in a Buddhist temple.*

Opposite: *An elaborate gilded and bejeweled Buddhist statue.*

Confucius (551–479 BC) is often called the 'king without a crown.' He lived in the state of Lu (in modern Shandong province) and set out to restore the way of life advised by the ancient sages, advocating disciplined behavior, within the context of the family, in order to create an ordered society. His wisdom had a great influence over many Asian countries. Confucius had no intention of setting up a new religion but, in time, a cult emerged with its own temples and eventually Emperor Wu (156–87 BC) made Confucianism the official state philosophy and core of education. The Confucian state was largely tolerant of the various religions that flourished and today most faiths draw on the Confucian tradition and still revolve around personal development and are family-orientated. Many people worship their ancestors and Chinese folk religion respects gods and spirits drawn from myths and legend, which are remembered at many colorful festivals.

Taoism (translated as 'The Way') follows the wise teachings of Lao Tzu, a (possibly mythical) philosopher born about 2500 years ago. He researched many ideas in the imperial library — and the stories tell how he studied scrolls there. Saddened by the evil he witnessed all around him, Lao Tzu set off into the desert on a water buffalo but, before he left, a gatekeeper at the Great Wall persuaded him to record all his ideas for posterity.

Not so long ago, the Emperor of China was still believed to be the Son of Heaven and, although not a deity, was expected to mediate between the forces of Heaven and Earth. The last Emperor was P'u Yi, born 1906, who inherited his imperial title when only two years old. In 1911, rebellion swept through the country and by 1912 the five-year-old Emperor had been forced to renounce his throne — but he continued to live behind the mighty walls of Beijing's Forbidden City, cared for mainly by eunuchs. He was briefly declared Emperor again in 1917 and then faced a succession of false hopes of restoration and betrayals. He remained a puppet manipulated by others until he died in 1967.

During the years after World War II, China came to be dominated by Communism. The Chinese Communist Party was founded here in 1921. Over 12 months, some 100,000 men and their families crossed high mountains, deep gorges, and swamps to reach a haven in Shaanxi. Possibly only about 30,000 survived the 8000 mile (12,800km) trek. After more than 20 years of civil war, Mao Tse-tung finally led the Communists to victory in 1949, proclaiming the People's Republic of China.

Above: *In this Chinese temple a row of golden Buddha statues, set in decorative niches, are surrounded by countless tiny niches, many with statues inside.*

Opposite: *In the Temple of Six Banyan Trees in Guangzhou, Amitabha is one of three ancient 19ft (6m) high statues that represent present, past, and future.*

Left: *Although incense burners may be used in Europe, they were always far more widespread in eastern temples. This ornate brass example stands in a bright red temple setting.*

Right: *A silver portrait of Chairman Mao (Mao Tse-tung) graces a red badge. Badges carrying his younger image appeared before China's Cultural Revolution in the late 1960s.*

Martial arts and Chinese medicine

Today many Chinese also follow such ancient practices as astrology and feng shui by which they hope to achieve harmony with the environment by the judicious arrangement of everything around them. This also involves weather, astronomy, and geomagnetism and is believed to strongly influence health, wealth, and relationships with other people.

Legend claims that Chinese martial arts began in 2698 BC during the reign of the Yellow Emperor, a famous ruler and general who wrote lengthy treatises on medicine, astrology, and the martial arts. Certainly, martial training has played an important role throughout Chinese history. During the Tang Dynasty (AD 618-907) warriors and officers were selected through their prowess in martial competition. Sword dances, wrestling, kick boxing, fencing, sparring, and spear training have all contributed to the development of stylized self defense, with control of the mind being as important as the

development of the muscles. These are not only highly demanding sports but also refined and complex art forms.

Traditional Chinese medicine (or TCM) incorporates many different therapeutic and diagnostic practices that have developed over thousands of years. Treatments include herbal medicine, massage, and acupuncture — all of which have now percolated to the West where they are highly regarded by many people. Medical practice in China places great store on the meridian system in the human body. This is envisaged as a network of channels through which chi (or qi) energy is circulated. This can be modified during acupuncture by the insertion of fine needles at strategic acupoints on the meridians.

The five elements are very important in TCM too. Earth is to do with fertility and growth, and so relates to digestion, stomach, and spleen. Water represents the bladder, kidneys, and how fluids move through the body and are dissipated. Fire represents energy embodied in the heart and small intestine and the circulation of fluids — and joy. Wood stands for roots and strength and is concerned with the liver, gall bladder, blood storage, and the smooth flow of qi. Metal is a conductor and so is concerned with the lungs (that help conduct energy through the body) and the large intestine that conducts waste, excreting both bile and anger.

Above: The teacher of this young kung-fu student is demonstrating the controlled and safe breaking of a brick on the boy's head.

Above and opposite: A young man practices Wushu (martial arts). During the Tang Dynasty (AD 618-907) warriors were selected and officers promoted through martial competition.

Above: The Chinese have been making paper lanterns for 2000 years. At New Year, large numbers of new bright red lanterns are used to decorate streets, houses, businesses — and temples.

Background: The Chinese flag consists of a red background decorated with golden yellow stars — hot flaming colors that reflect the fire and enthusiasm of this vibrant nation.

Fire — the element

China has long been a place where new ideas thrive, where the best are revered and long retained. The element of fire has, throughout the centuries of this longest-enduring civilization, kindled the light of inspiration and creativity. The rest of the world has admired — and sometimes envied — the inventiveness and wisdom of the Chinese people. To some outsiders, China has seemed an enigma, a place of many secrets but, as this chapter has illustrated, the Western world has absorbed, and benefited from, many of the discoveries ignited by a Chinese spark of inspiration!

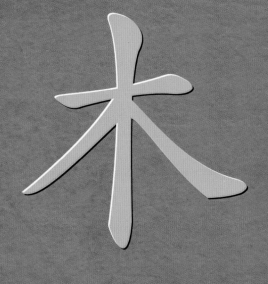

WOOD

While forests generally shrink all around the globe through the effects of deforestation, China, although not a heavily wooded nation, has made an enormous effort in recent years to replant trees. The coverage has risen constantly for almost two decades to create what is one of the largest artificial afforested areas in the world. Since 1990, forests in China have been growing by 1.2 percent (or 7000sq miles/18,100km^2) every year – a figure claimed to be the globe's highest.

Left: An amazingly versatile medium – here, in this antique work, wood has been intricately carved and decorated.

Forests and trees

There are now thought to be more than 193,000sq miles (500,000km²) of cultivated forest in China, with an overall forest coverage of about 618,000 to 676,000sq miles (1.6 to 1.75 million km²) — some 18 percent of the country's total area. The international average however — to put this in perspective — is 34 percent.

All these trees contribute in some part to the world's carbon dioxide 'sink' as well as proving a valuable natural resource. Moreover, they provide a rich habitat for huge numbers of birds and animals, while bamboo and felled timber has a multitude of uses, including making paper.

While the proportion of wooded areas in China — when set against the country's immense acreage — is not vast, this is not a bland sweep of green. There are around 2800 different tree species to be found here, including rare and unusual ones, such as the dawn redwood and the ginkgo *(Ginkgo biloba)*, a unique tree with no close living relatives. A living fossil, the ginkgo is considered the oldest tree species to survive on Earth, with a lineage dating back some 270 million years to the Permian period. It flourished in the Middle Jurassic around 170 million years ago and so witnessed many dinosaur species come and go long before humans came on the scene. It is now a national symbol of China, said to reflect the nation's long history, culture, and indomitable spirit.

China's natural forests are concentrated in the southwest and in the northeast where a tree belt wraps around the Greater and Lesser Hinggan mountains and the Changbai (or Baekdu) Mountains on the North Korean border. These are China's greatest natural forest areas, with timber reserves that account for over one-third to half of the national output.

Changbai (or Baekdu) Mountain is the highest peak in the Changbai range — the legendary birthplace of the imperial family who founded the Qing Dynasty (1644–1911) and the Manchu state. Literally translated, the name means *Perpetually White Mountain Region.* Cold dry winters are the norm here with continuous permafrost on the highest peaks, alpine meadows, and rocky slopes — but no glaciers. Mountain birch and larch, spruce, fir, and Korean pine grow on the higher rugged terrain with maple, elm, and Amur linden flourishing lower down. Temperate hardwood forest is found farther below with more poplar and birch. The forests in the Changbai Mountains are the richest in variety in northeast China.

Above: *The foliage glows golden in a birch forest on Changbai mountain in Jilin province.*

Opposite: *China now has many forest reserves; in this rugged area, trees flourish among towering cliffs.*

Left: *A photographer in a beautiful forest reserve stands among the foliage on a viewing platform at the edge of a precipitous cliff.*

Below: *The China Forest and Trade Network (launched 2005) aims to eliminate illegal logging and preserve threatened forests.*

Bottom: *A misty scene in Zhangjiajie national park where jagged sandstone pillars and peaks tower above thick forest in the valley.*

Located near the northeastern border of China, in Inner Mongolia, the volcanic Greater Hinggan Mountains boast abundant forests, rivers, and dormant volcanoes. Mixed forests of pine and deciduous broadleaf trees cover extensive low-lying hills where Siberian (or Manchurian) tigers prowl and the renowned medicinal plant ginseng *(Panax ginseng)* occasionally flourishes in the conifer forest's understory. This highly esteemed medicinal plant, once found in many places in northeast China, has been severely depleted in recent decades because of logging, forest fires, and over-eager collection of its parsnip-like root for medicinal purposes. It may be extinct in many of its former haunts. Reputedly an anticarcinogen, it is also said to increase energy and virility, while reducing stress.

Manchurian mixed forests occupy lower hills in Jilin, Liaoning, and Heilongjiang provinces. Here are found both deciduous broadleaf forests with oaks, ashes, birches, Manchurian elms, maples, and Manchurian walnut trees. Coniferous forests are full of tall straight-trunked Korean pines, firs, and spruces while woodlands on the east slope of the Greater Hinggan Mountains include fine birches, elegant poplars, willows, and Mongolian oaks — with conifer forests dominated in sandier regions by the Scots pine with its scaly layered bark and distinctive clumps of foliage.

The Laotu Dingzi reserve supports primary forests of Japanese yew, which has a short trunk and finely textured fragrant bark while the Jingbo Lake nature reserve in Heilongjiang province includes mixed forests with conifers and deciduous broadleaf trees, such as maples and oaks. In the Hengduan Mountains, a range that runs south from the Himalayas, red sandal grows — and nanmu, a type of wood frequently used for boat building, woodwork on buildings, and as an art medium. The southeastern forests of China cover the vast hilly areas south of the Qinling Mountains and Huaihe River and east of the Yunnan-Guizhou plateau. These are mainly cultivated areas with moso bamboos, masson pines, lacquer trees, and tea plants.

Right: This contorted, windswept pine grows on Sanqing mountain, a sacred place for Tang-Dynasty Taoists known as The Land of Peach Blossoms, where three peaks (Yujing, Yuhua, and Yuxu) represent three gods worshiped in Taoism. It is said that faithful Taoists will ascend to Heaven if they climb the huge stone at Yujing's peak.

Protecting forests and wildlife

To help reduce the impact of sandstorms and prevent soil erosion, China has constructed many so-called 'shelter forests' in the north, northeast, and northwest of the country, along the middle and upper reaches of the Chang River, as part of the plan to plant new forests on the plains and by the coast on the Taihang Mountains. More than 98 percent of the coastline in southwest China's Guangxi Zhuangzu autonomous region has been afforested to create a strong shield to protect against typhoons and reduce the impact of any future tsunamis.

Siberian tigers *(Panthera tigris altaica)* once ranged from the far east of Russia through Manchuria and into the southern part of the Korean peninsula but they are now very rare indeed, although some may be spotted in the Changbai Mountains of Jilin province and the forests of northern Heilongjiang province. The South China tiger *(Panthera tigris amoyensis)* is the most critically endangered of the five remaining tiger subspecies with probably less than 20 individuals left in the wild in central and eastern China. The irony is that this vanishing tiger strain was probably the original 'blueprint' and the ancestor of all the world's various tigers — both today's species and several that have already become extinct.

Other important and protected mammals that roam in China's forests and scrubby cover include the small sable *(Martes zibellina)*, a very graceful marten-like carnivore but sadly one long hunted for its beautiful fur, especially the velvety black ones. Rare golden snub-nosed monkeys *(Rhinopithecus roxellana)* inhabit the bamboo jungles, coniferous forests, and rhododendron thickets of south-central and western China. Unfortunately, this species is listed as endangered because it is hunted intensively for its fiery orange pelts and other body parts that are used in traditional medicines.

Other endangered forest dwellers

Many deer are also found in the forests. Sika *(Cervus nippon)* usually live in mixed deciduous forests and are elegant-looking animals with long slender legs, dark chestnut brown summer coats, and a distinctive large white rump patch that they sometimes fluff out as a signal to others if they suspect any danger nearby.

Musk deer *(Moschus moschiferus)* are solitary shy animals. The males have long upper canines but neither sex bears antlers. A musk gland in the genital region of the males creates a long-lasting odor that is used in perfume. Musk deer have long been hunted for this musk pouch and populations are now considered critically endangered. They live in both wet and mountainous forests. Red deer *(Cervus elaphus)*, named for their beautiful russet color, have large impressive antlers and prefer to live in open woodlands rather than dense forests. Xinjiang autonomous region is home to a central Asian subspecies of the red deer, the highly endangered Yarkand deer *(Cervus elaphus yarkandensis)*.

Black or hairy-fronted muntjac *(Muntiacus crinifrons)* deer dwell in forests in the middle and lower reaches of the Chang River valley. These are shy creatures whose numbers are falling fast, as are those of predatory wolves and jackals that once thrived in Hunan. The Shanghai Zoo plans to house a large pack of wolves in order to save this highly intelligent species from extinction. The penetrating howl of the timber wolf *(Canis lupus)* helps it to communicate effectively over great distances, even in thick forests. Bear-like wolverines *(Gulo gulo)* hunt in China's cool temperate coniferous forests too, but these are actually members of the weasel family.

Above: *The compelling gaze of a rare Siberian tiger.*

Opposite: *Elegant red deer are found in China's open woodland.*

Above: The sika deer suckles her hungry nuzzling fawn. She has a rich brown coat that is attractively spotted in summer but almost black (with indistinct spots) in winter.

Left: The powerful jaws of a wolverine can crunch through the meat and bone of its prey even in icy wintertime when its meal may be retrieved from a buried cache frozen solid.

Opposite: The unmistakable howl of a timber wolf is audible up to 6 miles (10km) away and helps it to stay in contact with the rest of the pack — and to warn off rivals.

Below: There may be as few as ten critically endangered Amur leopards left in the wild in the temperate forests of China's northern extremes. The thick golden-orange fur of these magnificent big cats helps them to survive the freezing winter weather here — and in Russia where they are also found.

Chinese cats include the leopard *(Panthera pardus)*, with its beautiful spotted coat that helps to camouflage it in the lowland forests and mountain scrubs. Usually nocturnal, by day the leopard will rest in dense vegetation on the branch of a tree or among rocks. The Amur leopard *(Panthera pardus orientalis)* that lives on the borders of Russia and China is considered to be one of the most critically endangered big

cats in the world, with perhaps just a few individuals remaining in the Jilin province of northeast China. The North Chinese leopard *(Panthera pardus japonensis)* has darker orange background fur than other leopards, with large rosettes that sometimes enclose a separate spot. This again is a very rare large cat and the wild population is categorized as endangered.

Superbly marbled Asian golden cats *(Pardofelis temminckii)* live in South China's forests and often seem to have more distinctive markings here than do some of their relatives in other territories. They may be seen at altitudes of up to 10,000ft (3000m) in the Himalayas and like to prowl where the trees are interspersed with rocky areas that provide good vantage points as they hunt their prey, which includes rodents, lizards, and even small deer. In some parts of China they are known as *Shilului* — rock cats.

Mountain and forest habitats

In recent decades, the northern or Eurasian lynx *(Lynx lynx)* has been driven up into rocky mountain areas to escape from human disturbance but some do still live in more open woodlands, where they hunt mammals and small deer. Siberian ground squirrels nest in hollow tree trunks and rotting branches on the forest floor. China has announced plans to create a special squirrel park in Zhejiang province near the Lin'an Gorge where vast numbers of squirrels scurry about — as do spotted deer and endangered tree-dwelling pangolins, scaly little mammals that almost exclusively devour ants. They roam in the southern Chang River basin and will curl up into a ball like armadillos if frightened.

The mountain hare *(Lepus timidus)* — found in Xinjiang Uygur, Inner Mongolia, and Heilongjiang — lives in woodland or scrub areas. It is nocturnal and feeds on twigs, leaves, and grass. The impressive Asiatic black bear *(Ursus thibetanus)*, with its distinctive white crescent chest flash, is found in many regions — even roaming through the trees as far south as Hainan. They inhabit forested areas, particularly where trees thread around hills and mountains. Those found in the colder climes need to hibernate. These bears can balance proficiently on their hind feet and captive ones have been taught to dance.

Smaller woodland wildlife

A walk through the woods in China may also reveal various tree frogs, the Chinese jumping mouse, and the crested porcupine, an animal that is smaller than its African counterpart and has fewer quills over its rear end. Red wood ants mass in coniferous forests but are also found in some deciduous woodlands, living in colonies of some half a million individuals, where they can be observed foraging for food, killing other insects, and 'milking' honeydew from aphids, which is a staple part of their diet.

Left: A Eurasian lynx family snuggles up together but, except for mothers with cubs, the lynx usually lives a solitary life. Thick fur on their paws acts like winter 'snowshoes' helping them to maintain traction on icy terrain.

Above: Asiatic black bears are aggressive and likely to attack if startled. These powerful and impressive bears were hunted for their gall bladders and bile, once used in Chinese medicine.

Birdlife in the forests

Partridges and pheasants are a Chinese 'specialty' introduced to Europe long ago; there are many variations on the basic theme (partridges and quails are smaller members of the pheasant family). In the wild, they roost in trees and China's forests provide an excellent sheltered home to several partridges, such as the spectacular Sichuan partridge (*Arborophila rufipectus*). If you do manage to spot one, it flaunts a distinctively patterned head and breast, an orange ear-covert patch, and black-streaked white throat. Here too live mountain bamboo partridges (*Bambusicola fytchii*), Chinese bamboo partridges (*B. thoracicus*), and stocky red-and-orange Temminck's tragopans (*Tragopan temminckii*).

The beautiful golden (or Chinese) pheasant (*Chrysolophus pictus*) flashes its wonderful bright feathers in the forests of mountainous western China but is surprisingly hard to spot in the dense conifer cover. Reeves's pheasant (*Syrmaticus reevesii*) live in the evergreen forests of central and eastern China and this spectacular golden-colored bird is noted as having the bird kingdom's longest natural tail feathers — they can grow to 6.6ft (2m) in length.

Silver orioles (*Oriolus mellianus*) and Emei leaf-warblers (*Phylloscopus emeiensis*) live in China's tropical or tropical moist lowlands, while the gold-fronted fulvetta (*Alcippe variegaticeps*) is endemic to China's subtropical or tropical moist montanes (tropical mountain forests). The Emei Shan liocichla (*Liocichla omeiensis*) is a gray-and-olive babbler with prominent red wing-patches that is found in south-central Sichuan and northeast Yunnan. These are all rare birds, but China has a healthy population of many other fine, if rather more common, birds that merit the attentions of ornithologists. As well as the many waders and waterbirds found here, including gorgeous mandarin ducks and pheasant-tailed jacanas, there are (to cite just a few examples) buzzards, black kites, eagles and other birds of prey, cuckoos and kingfishers, hoopoes, woodpeckers, jays, and magpies. Flowerpeckers include fire-breasted types, while several kinds of tit, flycatchers, redstarts, tree-creepers, warblers (including bush and reed warblers), laughing thrushes, skylarks, rosefinches, and parrotbills are all found in, around or above the trees of China.

Right: Reeves's pheasants are named for British naturalist and businessman, John Reeves, who sent the first live specimens back to England from China in 1831.

Left: This ornate red and gold wood carving is in a Chinese temple. Animal representations, motifs, and themes have greatly influenced Chinese art, with sculpture, pottery, paintings, performing arts, and martial arts all embodying animal themes and symbols. Graphic representations of lions and dragons are especially prevalent.

Above: This gnarled ancient tree is lit by the golden afternoon sun in a Chinese courtyard — where often date, locust, clove, and pomegranate trees are planted, especially in Beijing's hutong *passageways around the Forbidden City. Pomegranates are popular because the mass of seeds in the fruit represents fertility and abundance. In China, a picture of a ripe open pomegranate is a popular wedding present.

Bamboo forests

Bamboo is an enormously important natural resource in China and is valued here as a symbol of longevity and resistance to hardship because it grows fast and tall, stays green all year round, and is tough and incredibly useful. In China the bamboo stands are not isolated patches but veritable jungles. It is actually a true grass but grows as a woody perennial. China supports over 500 species in 40 genera, almost half of the globe's total, and can claim more types and planted areas than any other part of the world. China has one quarter of the world's total acreage of bamboo forests, covering over 15,500sq miles (40,000km^2), half of which support moso bamboo (*Phyllostachys pubescens*) especially so in the man-made forests of the south and southwest China.

Different bamboos have different habits but, despite the precocious growth of some species, they may take 15 to 20 years to reach full size and often grow for many years — sometimes 40 or more — before producing seeds. Then they will flower, set seed, and promptly die. Some species achieve giant dimensions, producing new shoots that may grow over 3.3ft (1m) every day. One Japanese scientist recorded a growth spurt of nearly 4ft (1.2m) in 24 hours in a specimen of *ma-dake* bamboo.

In Sichuan, the bamboo forests have been given wonderfully evocative names, such as the Emerald Corridor and No Worry Valley, as well as the 46sq mile (120km^2) Bamboo Sea, a world-renowned bamboo reserve. In many ancient legends, dragons were associated with bamboo, while scholars — admiring the firm, erect growing habit of bamboo — linked it with upright behavior, good morals, and integrity. Hermits often chose to retreat into the bamboo forests, reveling in the peace and solitude there. One story tells how, long ago, upon the death of Shun, a ruler of ancient China, his two wives wept copious tears onto the bamboos by the river, leaving great wet spots on their leaves, and so, ever since, there have been mottled bamboos growing in southwest China.

During the Tang Dynasty (AD 618–907), poet Wang Wei described in a poem how he enjoyed: 'Sitting alone in the dark bamboo grove, I am playing my zither and singing alone. No-one would know in this dark wood. Only the bright moon for company.'

Most varieties of bamboo stay green all year round and so provide good shelter and a safe place to hide for many creatures. For birds, bamboo forests offer a secure place to raise their young. Indeed, farmers in southern China often let their chickens roam in forest areas and may combine the occupations of bamboo growing with raising poultry.

Bamboo serves as a prime habitat for giant pandas (*Ailuropoda melanoleuca*) for whom it is the favorite item on the menu. Sometimes they devour other leaves, berries, blossoms, and bird eggs but, mostly, they just spend hours on end enjoying the bamboo that comprises some 99 percent of their diet. The pandas eat the soft shoots, stems, and leaves. They have large teeth and strong jaws that help them to chew the tougher leaves and stalks, while a small, bony projection on the wrists provides an extra firm grip on stems. Bamboo is abundant but has poor nutritional value, which explains why pandas spend so long eating it every day to ensure they receive adequate nutrition.

Both giant pandas and red pandas (*Ailurus fulgens*) live in the cool temperate bamboo forests of Sichuan and Yunnan provinces and on the forested mountain slopes of the Chinese Himalayas. Both are endangered because of habitat loss through logging activities and the encroachment of agriculture: there are thought to be fewer than 2500 adult red pandas and only an estimated 2000 giant pandas living in the wild today.

Opposite above: *Giant pandas digest only about one-fifth of the huge quantity of bamboo they eat and will spend about 12 hours a day feeding. Pandas can eat most of the bamboo species found in their habitat. Although most giant pandas depend on about 10 different kinds of bamboo, they may feast upon more than 40 different species of the plant.*

Background: *There are many species of bamboo growing in China but only relatively few grow at the high altitudes where pandas live. Should all the bamboo die off in a region that supports wild pandas, as happens after their rare flowering, the animals may starve.*

Following pages: Bundles of tall bamboo canes (the world's fastest-growing plant) are usually set out to dry at the end of summer or in winter, when they are less likely to crack or split. Natural air-drying of the canes may take several months.

Versatile bamboo

Bamboo is both useful and highly adaptable, a resource from which many products can be made. Moreover, it is not just pandas that eat bamboo; humans relish it too. Its crisp, but tender, shoots are a great delicacy and the tips are added to countless soups and dishes in eastern countries. It can be made into pancakes with rice flour, and its leaves serve as wrappers for Chinese steamed dumplings called *zongzi*, adding to the flavor.

The chopsticks with which such delicacies are eaten may be made of bamboo too. So are very lightweight food steamers. Bamboo sap can be fermented to create cordial, liquor, or sweet wine and various medicinal products are derived from it and used in both Chinese herbal treatments and Indian Ayurvedic medicine. Black bamboo is a vital ingredient in a potion to treat kidney ailments, while its sappy secretion (called tabasheer) serves to treat coughs and asthma, as a cooling tonic, and even as an aphrodisiac.

Bamboo plays a significant role in China's economy and exports. At home, it is a vital building material: some of the larger bamboos, especially *Phyllostachys* species, are termed 'timber bamboos.' Once treated, this produces an excellent, hard, durable but light wood that can be used for scaffolding or as reinforcing rods for concrete. It often serves as the fabric of the actual buildings too — as well as being used to make an incredibly diverse mix of artifacts, including flooring, fences, tableware, furniture, toys, masks, hats, walking sticks, cutting boards, fans, pipes for smoking, baskets and cages, garden stakes, ski poles, baseball bats, and fishing rods. Flutes and other musical instruments have been made of bamboo, too, including the dizi, a simple traditional wind instrument.

Sharpened to a fine point, bamboo splints can be used as tattoo or knitting needles. Its fibers can be processed into knitting yarn or a fabric used to make rugs, sheets, towels, and clothing. Traditional weapons, such as rockets and fire arrows, were all made from it, as were canoes. Rope-makers traditionally cut bamboo into thin strips to be woven into ropes that were braided together into a strong cable. In the 13th century, Marco Polo described how fishermen used tough bamboo ropes to tow boats. Some of the earliest suspension bridges spanned deep ravines and rushing rivers and they were secured by cables woven from bamboo strips. Cabled bamboo strips held up the great Anlan suspension bridge over the River Minjiang at Guanxian, a marvel of the ancient world that survived from about the 3rd century AD until 1975, when steel cables finally replaced the bamboo.

Bamboo was being utilized in China over 4000 years ago and in the Yin and Shang Dynasties (1500s BC to 1066 BC) it served to make arrowheads. By the 700s BC, strips of it were used as a messenger-carrying medium with words carved on them, while in the Qin Dynasty (221-207 BC) people made bamboo pens. By the 3rd century AD paper was being created from it and during the Song Dynasty (AD 960–1279). The scholar Su Shi lauded its usefulness in this way: 'bamboo shoot for food, bamboo tile for house making, bamboo hat for rain sheltering, bamboo wood for fuel, bamboo skin for clothing, bamboo paper for writing and bamboo shoes for foot wearing … we cannot do without bamboo.'

It still serves as medium for art and handicrafts, is sometimes carved to make decorative pieces of artwork, and its fibers are used to form high-quality hand-made paper. Long ago, in the last two centuries BC, characters were scratched onto slips of green bamboo that were strung together with silk strands or sinew to create the first books.

Above: *This renowned Chinese tea,* Pu-erh, *is aged to improve its flavor and may be wrapped in bamboo shoot husks or bamboo leaves during this process.*

Opposite above: *The Chinese use 45 billion pairs of disposable chopsticks a year, most of them made of bamboo.*

Opposite below: *Food can be cooked and served in lightweight bamboo steamers, staying hot in the warm baskets — perfect for* dim sum *dishes.*

172

Right: An old umbrella with intricate bamboo spokes. The Chinese made the first umbrellas some 2000 years ago — originally of silk, then paper. Later they were waxed to resist rain.

Above: Bamboo scaffolding is often used in China and sometimes the floors, and even entire buildings, are made of bamboo. It may even be the fabric for construction workers' hard safety hats!

Timber at home

While Chinese bamboo furniture has been made for many hundreds of years and is still popular today, it was timber that both preceded and exceeded it, being used for high-quality furniture and the finest chairs and stools by the 1100s. The most prosperous late Ming Dynasty (1368–1644) is considered by many to be the Golden Age of Chinese furniture, especially in the rich coastal cities where the furniture exhibited superb craftsmanship — simple but elegant, with sweeping lines and curved backrests. The excellent standard of joinery made the use of any nails or glue superfluous, while metal additions (such as handles, hinges, and lock plates) were designed to be just as graceful as the carpentry.

Craftsmanship and associated skills were passed down through the generations as artisans produced countless beautiful pieces that were far more advanced than anything being made in Europe at the time. Most Ming furniture was made of timber harvested from indigenous trees such as pine, elm, and zelkova (southern elm). However, once the ban on imports had been lifted in 1567, precious tropical hardwoods were used. The beautiful wood and its grain were always evident, even though many pieces were finished with carved lacquer or inlaid with red or black lacquer — or perhaps mother of pearl or agate. The far more opulent painted and lacquered items arrived later.

During the early Qing Dynasty (1644–1911) the furniture that was made for the ruling classes was similar to Ming styles with simple classic lines and finishes. By the end of the 1700s, however, more angular forms and rather over-ornate carvings were the order of the day for the wealthy buyer, although in the ordinary village home and town house, people still sat or ate or kept their possessions in simply styled furniture — albeit often lacquered in red or black and decorated with appropriate symbols, patterns, or landscapes. These styles persisted in China into the early 20th century, being distinguished by various distinct regional differences.

Throughout the centuries and into the present day, Chinese carpentry has been executed and finished with great care, whether for exquisite palace beds, elegant screens and dressing-tables, or the simplest barrel or bench. Over the years, many Europeans have imported beautifully proportioned tables and chairs, chests of drawers, trunks, and desks, and whether the furniture is elegant lacquerware or simple traditional style, it is made with fine attention to detail.

Above: Superbly detailed ancient wood carving in Sichuan.

Opposite: An antique wood carving showing traditional figures.

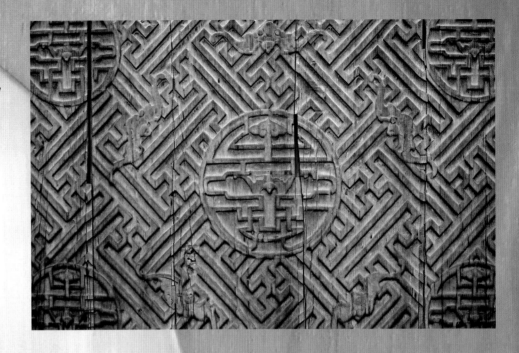

Background: This old Chinese cupboard door exhibits the fine craftsmanship of Chinese carpentry with exquisite finishing touches.

Opposite: A sitting room where the traditional Chinese chairs are beautifully carved, adding elegance but without appearing excessively opulent.

Above: Intricate carving creates a maze-like effect on a wooden door in Beijing. In this modern city, many traditional handicrafts can be found in the details that Westernization has left untouched.

Below: The vibrant blue paint on this house wall and the brightly colored rickshaw serve to emphasize the sturdy, wooden paneled door, decorated with beautifully rendered calligraphy.

Long ago, it was not just furniture that was built of timber. Wooden pagodas were raised too, such as the Shakya timber pagoda built in 1056 at the small Fogong monastery in Shaanxi. This is the oldest pagoda and largest timber tower in China that exhibits the classical octagonal shape. It has five stories, each with an external gallery and is about 220ft (67m) tall and 100ft (30m) in diameter. It has withstood both earthquakes and artillery bombardment for nearly 1000 years.

In even earlier times, primitive people in China built their homes from branches and thatch raised over a shallow pit or a platform of wooden poles. In legend, they were taught these skills by the demigod named Youchaoshi and they called these homes 'nests.' Earth was packed around them to add to their strength and improve insulation and to help prevent the wood from catching fire. As Chinese culture developed, so wood became the material from which many different kinds of homes were made. Musical instruments also were often made of wood — the pipa lute, the erhu (a bowed instrument rather like a two-stringed violin) often used at the Beijing Opera and many others, often beautifully carved like the horse-headed fiddle. Large drums were once made from hollow tree trunks, often painted red, as drums still are today in China.

Opposite: *Pagodas were mostly built of wood, as were other ancient Chinese structures. Wooden pagodas are highly resistant to earthquakes, and they are often richly decorated or gilded like this fine example in a park in Hong Kong.*

Below: *The superb curves of this wooden Chinese temple, adorned with 'roof guardian' figures, sweep toward the sky.*

Following pages: *Detail of an amazing wooden ceiling in Beijing's Summer Palace, an extravagant explosion of detail, color, and rich patterned ornamentation.*

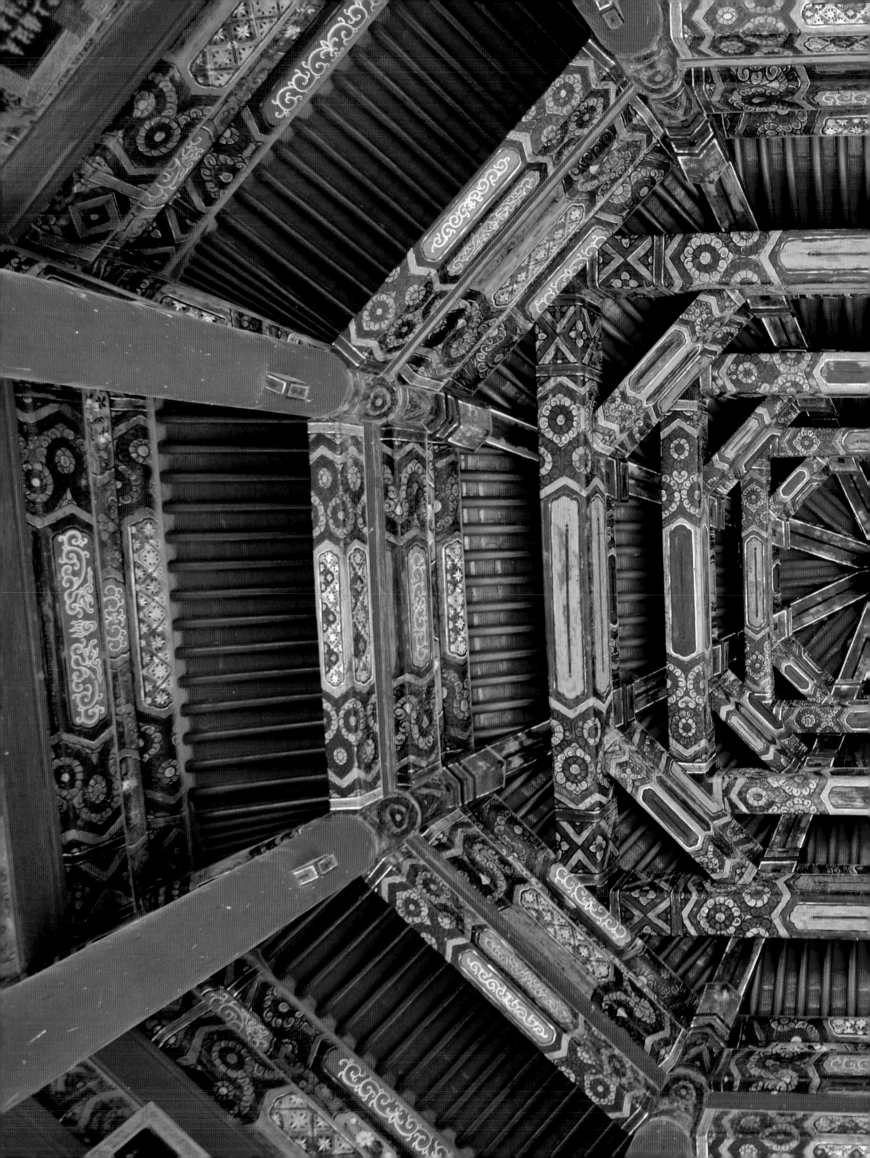

Trees in miniature: penjing and pun-sai

Chinese legends tell how long ago a Han emperor created a miniature landscape of his empire complete with tiny hills, valleys, rivers, lakes, and trees. It was set in his courtyard so that he could watch over it from his palace window. Anyone found copying this art form was put to death.

Another story tells how Chinese poet and civil servant Guen-ming grew miniature chrysanthemums in pots in the 4th century AD and then, some 200 years later, Tang Dynasty growers began to experiment further with this notion.

Landscaped arrangements of miniature trees and rockeries known as *penjing* originated in China over 2000 years ago and the Chinese were cultivating single specimen trees in pots, without any landscaping, over 1000 years ago, a kind of bonsai, albeit in a very simple way, which was then called *pun-sai*. The fascination arose when these dwarf specimens with their minute foliage and gnarled stunted trunks were often seen to resemble animals, birds, and dragons. Many myths and legends developed along with the skills, and so Chinese bonsai developed into a highly imaginative craft in which fiery dragons and coiled serpents were as much a part of the design as the miniaturized trees.

In 1972, wall paintings were discovered in the tomb of Prince Zhang Huai of the Tang Dynasty (he died in AD 706) showing servants carrying a miniature landscape and trees in pots that would appear to be *pun-sai* specimens. It was with the Chinese invasion of Japan in the 14th century that the art of bonsai spread to that country.

Above: Growing miniature trees in pots began in China 1000 to 1600 years ago and spread to Japan in the 14th century where the art is known as bonsai.

Above and opposite: Monks, scholars, and high officials crafted the first Chinese miniature trees, called penjing, whose twisted trunks often mimicked dragons, animals, and birds.

Creating with paper

The very earliest paper discovered was found in Fufeng county, Shaanxi, and was made from hemp during the Western Han Dynasty (206 BC–AD 29). 'Real' paper, however, did not put in its appearance until its invention by Ts'ai Lun in AD 105 (see also page 120). Bamboo paper became popular some six centuries later in the Tang Dynasty (618–907). Today China's best-known quality paper is probably the soft white Xuan paper; smooth, absorbent, and durable, it is made in Jing county, Anhui province, and is the one most used in painting and calligraphy here. To satisfy the Eastern aesthetic sense, choosing the right paper for the task at hand is very much a part of the artistic process.

The art of Chinese paper cutting may well have been developed by nobles in royal palaces who were looking for a way to pass the long hours and had access to what was then such a precious commodity. Between the 7th and the 13th centuries, paper cutting with knives and scissors created many incredibly delicate decorations and lanterns for celebrations and festivals. Eventually it became such an important and prized skill that prospective brides were required to prove their accomplishment before their marriage.

Today paper cutting is often used to represent the Chinese zodiac symbols and/or animals (bats are an especially lucky subject), as well as amazingly delicate flowers and as flourishes on gift wrappings. Decorating a doorway or entrances with paper cut-outs is supposed to bring good luck to the household.

Paper lanterns are often some of the first objects that children learn to create as paper cut-outs. In China they can be superb objects, beautifully colorful, decorative, and intricate. They certainly add to the gaiety of many festivals. There are five classifications: the Baby's Bottom is the miniature style that is associated today with the lanterns even young Westerners make at Christmas. The second class is called the Rolling Paper and this is represented by the high cylindrical lanterns that often decorate restaurants and bars. The third class is the Big Red or Tomato Light and is a round, classic-style, medium-sized lantern. The fourth class, called Crystal Magic, takes a geometric form with many square and triangular facets. The last, Buddha's Gastronomy, are the largest lanterns that often decorate temples and festival settings. Lanterns are so popular in China that a special holiday is dedicated to them — Lantern Festival.

Above: *Paper lanterns seem to encapsulate China's inventive spirit.*

Left and opposite: *The most skilled cut-paper designs achieve an amazing degree of delicate intricacy.*

The art of Zhe Zhi or Chinese paper folding, as opposed to paper cutting, arose shortly after the invention of paper and predated Japanese origami that was not developed for another five centuries, after AD 600. In China, the art was developed and refined in the creation of many simple but elegant forms. Today generally it focuses on inanimate objects, such as pagodas, hats, fruit, and boats, as opposed to the Japanese styles that specialize in animals and birds.

Paper can also be used to make wonderful kites — and masks too, such as the incredibly evocative Bejing Opera masks. Despite its French name, papier mâché actually originated in China where, back in the Han Dynasty (206 BC–AD 220), it was used to make pot lids and, amazingly, spears and helmets, toughened by many layers of lacquer. During the 8th-century wars, some captured Chinese prisoners were sent to Arabian-dominated Samarcanda and there taught the local craftsmen the art of making paper and papier mâché.

Of course paper and wood are also used in the creation of the many board games that originated in China, as well as the boxes in which to store the pieces — whether for Mah-jong, solitaire, Chinese checkers, or Xiangqi — a game of Chinese chess that originated some 2000 years ago.

Above: *Traditional wooden Chinese chess* (Xiangqi) *pieces represent rooks (chariots), knights (horses), elephants (bishops or ministers), mandarins (advisors, assistants, or guards), cannons, pawns (soldiers) and one king (or general).*

Right: *Papier-mâché Beijing Opera masks create a startlingly dramatic impact; China has been using a material similar to papier-mâché for centuries.*

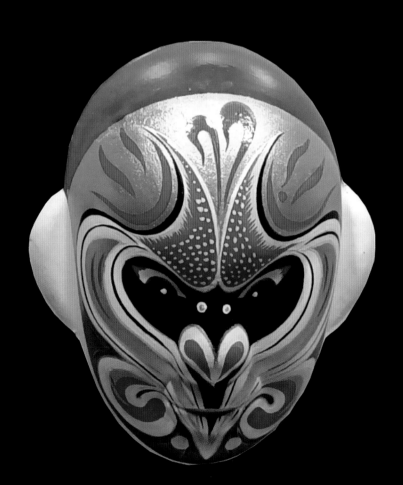

Wood — the element

In Chinese philosophy, wood feeds fire and parts earth. Its greatest attributes are its strength, flexibility, warmth, and generosity. It is associated with the sense of sight, the colors green and brown, birth and springtime and the Azure Dragon of the East — a constellation and mythical creature depicted as snake-like, wingless, and four-clawed. The element wood seeks to grow and expand: with the increased forest cover in China now, it should enjoy a better than ever opportunity to do so in this culture that expresses itself so eloquently through the many faces of wood.

Background: *Sanqing mountain — trees and bamboo feature strongly in China's landscape and provide a rich wildlife habitat, as well as timber that can be used to create so many things, from lofty pagodas and temples to furniture, delicate boxes, and the finest sheets of paper.*

METAL

In China the fifth element is metal: metal chops wood … and through the interplay of these materials buildings rise, towns and cities grow, while roads and bridges loop in an intricate network to link them. Today China has a total urban population of 540 million living in over 20,000 towns and 600 cities (49 of which are inhabited by more than a million people). Metal has provided the critical underpinning for so many of these developments.

***Left:** Golden metal lion heads with Oriental-shaped eyes and heavy brows gaze out inscrutably from the handle fittings of an ancient vessel in Beijing's Forbidden City.*

The fifth element

In this chapter, metal also represents the minerals in the earth. Modern high-rises seem to defy the force of gravity but nature itself can sometimes be wildly extravagant too even without any human interference. For example, in Yunnan in the southwest, the limestone pillars of the Stone Forest create a spectacular landscape of pillars, turrets, and jagged spires that reach for the sky.

The Bronze Age

The use of metal for tools was fundamental to the establishment of Chinese civilization. During the Bronze Age, which began in China in around 2000 BC, people discovered many metals that could be mined and soon learned how to smelt copper and tin to make bronze weapons, tools, and vessels. Once farmers could produce sufficient food for more than their immediate family, a more structured society with longer term strategic aims could emerge. Miners, bronzesmiths, potters, and builders began to set about their various tasks while soldiers went to war, for which they needed metal weapons.

By 1700 BC, the Chinese Bronze Age culture had evolved and extended along the banks of the Huang River in northern China. Here warring Shang rulers rode out from their walled cities to do battle, while workers within used bronze to make more peaceful implements, such as containers, bells, drums, cooking vessels, cups, and caldrons. In many cultures, bronze was first used for tools and weapons but in China it served primarily to make majestic vessels for state ritual and ancestor worship. Shang Dynasty artists decorated their goods — whether masks or vessels — with spiral patterns and animal forms, such as elephants, rams, birds, dragons, owls, tigers, bulls, snakes, and rhinoceroses. Later Zhou and Han Dynasty bronzes were often patterned with gold, silver, or turquoise inlays.

In Shang times, kings would order animal and human sacrifices as funerary offerings and, when a powerful royal court member died, his wives, servants, bodyguards, horses, and dogs might well be slain and buried with him. By the Zhou Dynasty (1122–256 BC), however, clay substitutes began to replace human sacrifices. In 1928, scientific excavations of an ancient burial site began at Anyang, the last Shang Dynasty capital. Regal tombs were found containing a hoard of superb bronzes, fine pottery, bronze vessels and mirrors, marble animals, jade carvings, and ivory cups inlaid with turquoise.

Opposite: Delicate gold patterning adorns this rotund bronze rhinoceros sculpture from the Han Dynasty. The powdered horns of real rhinos were used in traditional Chinese medicine.

Above: Ancient Chinese incense burners were often very elaborate. This bronze example has relief designs adorned with jade- and amber-colored decorative inserts.

The Terra-Cotta Warriors

Close to Xi'an lay the tomb of China's first emperor, Qin Shihuangdi, the ruler of Qin who had united China some 11 years before his death — over 2200 years ago. The sinking of wells by farmers led to the discovery of the tomb in 1974 and when the underground chamber was eventually opened, one of the most amazing Bronze Age sites was revealed — this was the resting place of the Terra-Cotta Army. Here stood more than 7500 life-sized charioteers and cavalrymen, horses, striding infantrymen, and kneeling archers, made entirely of terra-cotta. Frozen in time, each figure had been cast in molds but with heads and hands made and fired separately and complete with individually modeled facial features, coiffures, and bronze armor. The figures were created, painted, and fitted with actual weapons by some 700,000 laborers. The ceiling of the huge mausoleum was studded with pearl stars while mercury 'rivers' flowed below to symbolize the waters of the Earth.

The Qin rule collapsed shortly after the First Emperor's death in 210 BC but now the awesome sight of his vast imperial bodyguard can still be seen standing in the museum that has been built around the burial site. It brings sharply into focus the extraordinary Chinese world of so long ago.

Above and right: Emperor Qin's Terra-Cotta Army was discovered near Xi'an in 1974. Qin unified the warring clans into one nation before assembling nearly 8000 figures to guard his tomb.

Following pages: This amazing array of life-size warriors and horses remained hidden for 2200 years. So far just three underground pits, totaling 236,800sq ft (22,000m²), have been uncovered.

Jade and other precious materials

After the Shang period, ritual vessels became increasingly important — they were used by priests and members of the nobility during ceremonial occasions, their rich surfaces inlaid with gold, silver, and precious stones. Iron did not appear in China until the 5th century BC but, even after its discovery, bronze remained in regular use.

Gold, silver, and bronze, however, never surpassed the spiritual dominance of jade — a highly valued material deemed to have magical powers and called the 'stone of Heaven.' Too hard to be cut, it was worked by laboriously wearing away the surface with harder stones, such as crushed garnets, until a smooth form emerged. It is associated with morality, grace, dignity, good health, and luck; only high officials of the Western Han Dynasty (206 BC–AD 9) were allowed to be buried alongside jade articles made from smooth glossy nephrite, the ancient jade used in rituals and adornment for some 9000 years in China, and said to be symbolic of Confucian virtue. The rarer mineral form of jade, jadeite, also called the 'king of jade,' only appeared much later during the early Qing Dynasty (after AD 1644).

The Imperial house provided jade carvers with workshops and soon their skills reached new heights and sophistication. Through the centuries jade has been used to make intricate scepters, belt buckles, hair ornaments, and jewelry — often intricately carved with the phoenix or dragon emblem that is reserved for nobility. It has also been used for statues, such as the Sitting and the Recumbent Buddhas in the Jade Buddha Temple in Shanghai, which are carved from sparkling crystal-clear white jade.

Opposite: Dramatic figures, resplendent with fine detail and rich colors, feature in a magnificent jade art relief at the Zhu Jia Jiao Museum of the Road of Silk.

Below: This elegant reclining Buddha, made of gleaming white jade, is in Shanghai's Jade Buddha Temple. This temple was built in 1928 to house two precious jade Buddha statues.

Background: *Glorious gold leaf adds richness to many works of art in China, especially in temples and palaces. Here a dramatically sculpted golden face gleams in brilliant surroundings.*

Above: *Sumptuous relief decorations create a beautifully symmetrical effect on a golden temple door in Beijing. Gold has long been used for secular purposes too, including coinage.*

Transport across China

The great landmass of China is crossed today by 12 principal arterial highways — five vertical and seven horizontal. They are part of the total of 2,162,371 miles (3.48 million km) of roads that crisscross the country. Another 2500 miles (4000km) of expressways are being constructed each year, their total length spreading tentacles across a network of some 28,210 miles (45,400km). This road network is the world's second longest after the United States — and all have been built since 1988. The 1250-mile (2000-km) Jingzhu Expressway is the nation's longest road.

China's railroad system covers some 47,224 miles (76,000km) and is one of the globe's busiest networks, transporting almost one quarter of the world's total rail traffic although it only boasts 6 percent of its tracks. China still has a few industrial steam locomotives in its inventory and several agile mountain railroads scramble up its difficult southeastern terrain.

Rickshaws were a popular form of transport during the 19th century but these man-powered, two-wheeled carts were ultimately replaced by cycle rickshaws and auto rickshaws. Man-pulled rickshaws are now returning to Beijing streets where they are arousing mixed reactions, having been outlawed for several decades by Chairman Mao and generally regarded as a symbol of subjugation.

China has been called the world's bicycle kingdom as there are some 300 to 500 million cycles here — about one for every three members of its population. They are often heavily laden, carrying three members of a family at once and are a major contributory cause of city traffic congestion. They remain the most popular form of personal transportation although car ownership is rapidly on the increase. In 2002, the Chinese demand for cars soared by 56 percent and, while this was something of a blip, sales are expected to increase by 10-20 percent annually.

Building bridges

China has many renowned bridges. Opening in 1968, the Nanjing Yangtze River Bridge was the first modern bridge to be built across this river. It was built without foreign assistance and so is a significant triumph for modern Chinese civil engineering. The 2000 Wuhu Yangtze River Bridge is China's longest highroad and railroad amphibious bridge at over 6 miles (10km) with a main span of about 1024ft (312m). Then the world's longest arch bridge — the

new Lupu Bridge with its amazing steel-trussed curved rib — opened in Shanghai in 2003 while the Runyang Bridge was commissioned in 2005. This is a double-bridge construction traversing the Chang downstream of Nanjing, its southern half is a suspension bridge with a main span of 4888ft (1490m) — China's largest suspension bridge and the world's third biggest. In 2007, the vast Hangzhou Bay Transoceanic Bridge opened officially off the eastern coast. It connects the municipalities of Shanghai and Ningbo. With its six-lane highway and overall length of 22 miles (36km), this is the world's longest 'ocean-crossing' bridge.

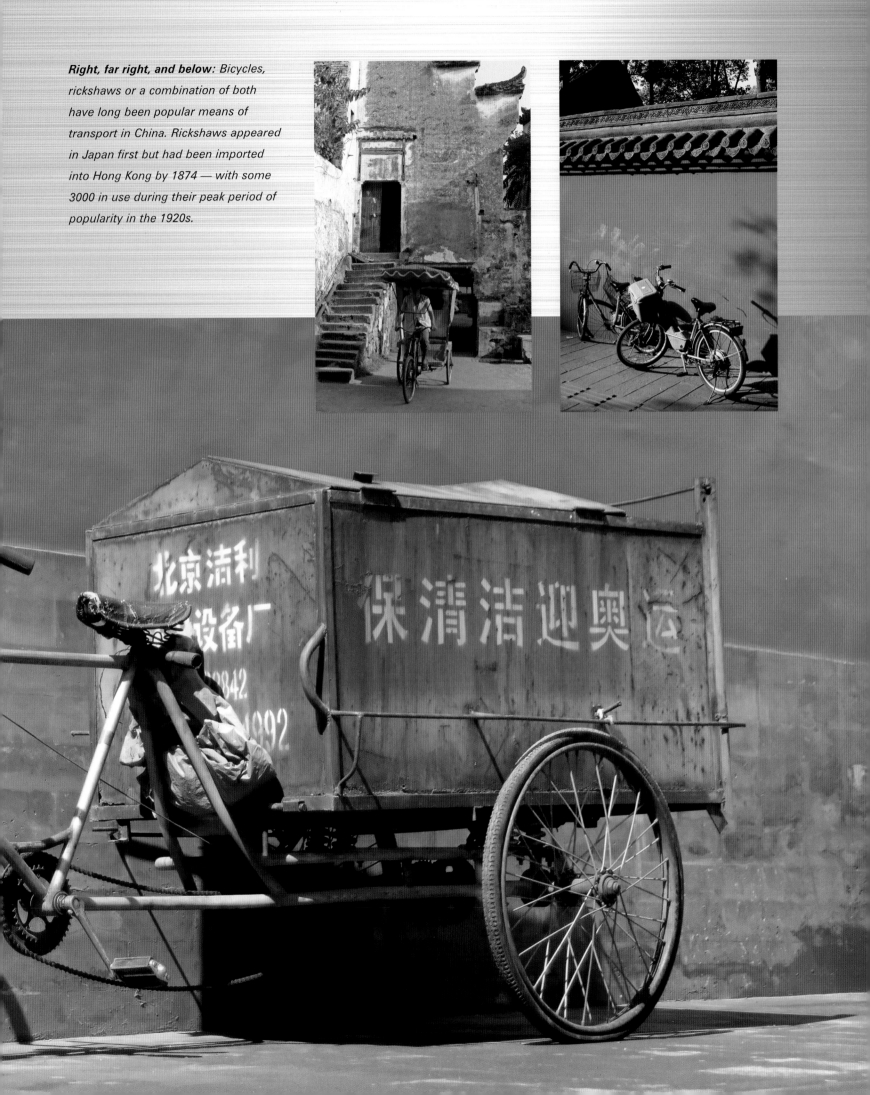

Right, far right, and below: Bicycles, rickshaws or a combination of both have long been popular means of transport in China. Rickshaws appeared in Japan first but had been imported into Hong Kong by 1874 — with some 3000 in use during their peak period of popularity in the 1920s.

Opposite above: The Jitong railroad, which was the world's last mainline all-steam railroad, tracks through the Hinggan mountains. It finally converted to diesel in 2005. Here a steam train is about to overtake an even older form of transport — a mule cart.

Opposite below: Shanghai boasts a futuristic magnetic levitation train — at 268mph (431kph) it is currently the world's fastest passenger train.

Background: The Qinghai-Tibet railroad line, the world's highest, reaches 16,640ft (5072m) above sea level as it carves through a barren, frozen landscape.

Much further back in time Lugou Qiao Bridge, also known as Marco Polo Bridge, was built in Beijing. This is one of the earliest segmented stone arch bridges with 485 beautifully carved stone lions crouching on its support pillars, no two beasts being alike. The original arches, built in 1192, were washed away in the 1600s and now the bridge is a composite of different eras. However, in essence it has been standing over the Yongding River for more than 800 years, and is particularly celebrated for the beautiful views of the moon that can be enjoyed from its vantage point during the mid-fall festival.

Most of the ancient bridges in China are of stone arch design. In Taishun county, Zhejiang province, streams and valleys between sharp mountain peaks are spanned by 900 covered bridges. Dongxi Bridge, with its four flying eaves, was erected during the Ming Dynasty (1368-1644); nearby is Beijian Bridge with 15 small covered 'rooms' forming a long covered passageway. These two 'sister bridges' are deemed to be China's most beautiful rainbow bridges. Extravagant Liuwen Bridge displays decorative opulence while Xianju Bridge in Wenzhou is a simpler ancient wooden arch with a large sweeping span.

The history of mighty road-building here dates back over 2000 years to the Silk Road, a trading caravan route which scholars believe first served as a link between nations in about 100 BC. Its overall extent (including some sea-miles) stretched some 4300 miles (7000km) between Rome and Xi'an, the capital of Shaanxi province.

It continued to be the major route for travelers and merchants until the 15th century when newly discovered sea routes to Asia offered an alternative. The Silk Road was not a single long track but formed a network of various routes, which forked and branched as they snaked across Asia. Porcelain, furs, gems, bronzes, gunpowder, paper, and the silk for which it is named traveled west from China along the Silk Road. Perfumes, black pepper, carnations and eastern spices were also transported west. Amber, ivory, carpets, horses, perfume, wool, cosmetics, and glass from Europe, Central Asia, Arabia, and Africa, as well as precious metals such as silver and gold, were transported east along this route. The opening of this trade route also facilitated the two-way exchange of culture, art, philosophy, and ideas.

Below: The Lugou Qiao (Reed Moat) or Marco Polo Bridge, which spans the Yongding River near Beijing, has 11 stone arches and features 485 carved stone lions. This was the starting point of the Chinese involvement in World War II, when Japanese and Chinese troops skirmished near the bridge in 1937.

Background: The Nanchang-Jiujiang highway and Nanchang Bridge in Jiangxi province encourage through-traffic to bypass the congested streets of Nanchang City.

Ancient cities

Beside the Silk Road on the northern rim of the Takla Makan Desert, at the foot of the Flaming Mountain and southeast of modern Turpan city, the 2000-year-old ruins of the oasis garrison city of Gaochang still make an impressive stand — a reminder of the days when so many merchant traders passed along this way. There are nine city gates, temples, towers, monks' homes, a grotto with fine murals, palace relics, and Khan's Castle — a square adobe pagoda standing on a high terrace to the north of the city.

Also near to Turpan, the ancient city of Jiaohe (Yarkhoto) has held sway for 2300 years. Set on a high cliff, it is one of the largest, oldest, and best-preserved earthen cities. It was home to some 700 households, 6500 residents and 865 soldiers. Although abandoned in the 1300s after it had been sacked by Genghis Khan's Mongols, much has survived, including houses, temples, streets, and graveyards.

A major port of the upper Chang River and often a stop-off point for visitors en route to the Three Gorges and its amazing dam, Chongqing or the Mountain City is now a major iron and steel producer, motorcycle manufacturing base, and shipbuilding center. All this industrialization seems to belie its ancient origins. It was given its present name by the Southern Song Emperor Guangzong in 1189 but long before, in the 13th century BC, it was the capital of the Ba Kingdom. About an hour's drive west of the city center, lies the ancient town of Ciqikou (Porcelain Harbor) which was a major porcelain producer during the Ming and Qing Dynasties. Here are found flagstone streets flanked by old timbered stores and restaurants.

Nearby is the port of Hechuan, with its white pagoda. This is the site of the longest continuous military campaign on Chinese soil, as Song forces held off Mongol invaders here for some 36 years (1243 to 1279). Also in the vicinity is the City of Ghosts (Fengdu) that has temples, shrines, and waxworks vividly and gorily depicting the sufferings of Hell.

Right: At Bezeklik, near Turpan, the Thousand Buddha Caves are a complex of temples, cave grottos, and rock-carved cliffs that date from the 400s to the 800s and house a multitude of Buddha statues and murals.

Opposite inset: Amid sheer cliffs and twisting rivers, Jiaohe's ancient earthen city ruins include 34 streets, 1389 houses, 53 Buddhist temples, and 316 ancient wells.

Mighty Shanghai

Set on the estuary of the Chang River, this is China's largest industrial city and one of the world's largest cargo ports, covering 2715sq miles (7037km²), with a population of 18.7 million. A fishing village that grew into a busy seaport from the mid 900s, it was granted its county status back in 1291 during the Yuan Dynasty. It attracted the unwelcome attention of Japanese pirates until a protective wall was raised in the 1500s.

Until relatively recent times the city was renowned for notorious slums, gangsters, and opium dens. Now Shanghai has reinvented itself as a modern city and vibrant port that attracts a more respectable class of visitor. The waterfront Bund (an Anglo-Indian term meaning 'muddy embankment') has a rich collection of early 20th-century architecture, as it is home to grand colonial buildings in fine neo-classical and art deco styles; here banks, trading houses, hotels, consulates, and clubs jostle shoulder to shoulder for space.

More recent building is concentrated in Pudong, described as Asia's Wall Street. It is primarily a finance and business center where the headquarters for multinational corporations and banks have given rise to an amazing skyline displaying many exotic skyscrapers, including the tallest tower in Asia, the Oriental Pearl TV tower, and the spectacular Jin Mao tower.

The 3-mile (5km) long Nanjing Road is one of China's busiest shopping streets with stores, restaurants, theaters, cinemas, and a constant throng of visitors. Making a sharp contrast to this bustling world, Shanghai's Jade Buddha Temple (see also page 198) houses several golden Buddhas as well as the remarkable jade statues for which it is named; the jewel-encrusted seated jade Buddha is particularly splendid.

The old city is the location of the Temple of the City's Gods (Chenghuang Miao) dating back to Ming times, the busy Yu Gardens bazaar, Huxington Teahouse built in 1784 by cotton merchants, and the 16th-century Yuyuan (or Mandarin's) Garden created in traditional Jianghan style. This features a garden within a garden, with carp-filled pools, dragon-lined walls, and zigzagging paths. An enormous rockery reflects in miniature south China's landscape with peaks, gorges, and caves.

Right: Shanghai's amazing illuminated skyline; the exquisite Oriental Pearl Tower, which features 11 differently sized spheres, rises 1536ft (468m) on the bank of Huangpu River.

Above: *Two giant skyscrapers — Shanghai World Financial Center, China's tallest structure since September 2007, rises next to the Jin Mao tower, mainland China's second highest.*

Opposite: *A sturdy door handle at Shanghai's Confucius temple. This was built in 1855 but the first temple was constructed here in 1267.*

Left: *The East Sculpture in Shanghai's Century Square; this is the largest square in Shanghai and has many fascinating sculptures and modern architectural structures.*

Below: *Pavilions in the 400-year-old Yuyuan Garden in Shanghai's old city. Following restoration the garden was opened to the public in 1961, and declared a national monument in 1982.*

Nanjing

The delightful city of Nanjing, the capital city of Jiangsu province, is set on the banks of the Chang, close to the Purple Mountain. Its cultural heritage stretches back to 472 BC. In AD 229, Wu Emperor Sun Quan made Nanjing his capital, a status it retained through several dynasties. Many centuries later, the Treaty of Nanjing, signed here in 1842, ceded Hong Kong to Britain for more than a century.

Highlights of the city include wide sweeping avenues, magnificent city walls, and two significant mausoleums: that of Sun Yat-sen (the father of the Republic of China — who led the 1911 revolution against the feudal system), a magnificent 20-acre (8ha) site — and the Ming Xiaoling mausoleum for Emperor Ming Taizu (or Zhu Yuanzhang) who founded the Ming Dynasty in 1368. This was raised under the heavy guard of 5000 military troops and it is said, perhaps fancifully, that when the emperor died, 13 identical funeral processions set out from as many different city gates so as to keep the real burial site of the emperor secret and so lower the risk of tomb raiding.

There is an excellent observatory on the slopes of Mount Zijinshan where the Confucius Temple is also found. This was originally constructed in 1034 to honor the great philosopher and educator. Rebuilt in 1984 after drastic war damage that occurred in 1937 when the Japanese attacked Nanjing, it is home to the largest figure of Confucius in China, as well as 38 jade, gold, and silver panels that depict his life story.

Right: Set against a mountain slope in Nanjing is the grand mausoleum of Sun Yat-sen (called the Father of Modern China) who, in 1911, founded the Republic. The 392 stone stairs that lead to the building represent the 392 million people, of all nationalities, living in China when the tomb was built.

Background: The Qinhuai, a branch of the Chang River, courses though the southern regions of ancient Nanjing. Here all the buildings and boats are brightly illuminated at night.

Yangzhou, Chengde, Chengdu, and Suzhou

Yangzhou has a history dating back nearly 2500 years and it has been a major economic hub, cultural center, and Grand Canal port since the Tang Dynasty (618-907). In the 800s, when it boasted an imperial palace, its strategic position on the Grand Canal made it an extremely prosperous city. It is thought that, during the 1280s, Marco Polo held a three-year post here as governor under the Mongol Emperor, Kublai Khan. Today the city is famous for its superb public bathhouses, busy wharfs, attractive haphazard old houses, and the tiny Tang Dynasty stone pagoda that stands in the shade of a 1000-year-old gingko tree. Nearby, beautiful Slender West Lake (a man-made lake created in the Tang Dynasty) is edged with weeping willows and pavilions. It inspired several poets of the period (see page 90). To the northwest lies the 5th-century Daming Temple where Jianzhen, a Tang Dynasty monk, studied before becoming a famous teacher of Buddhism, which, ultimately, he helped spread to Japan where he spent the final years of his life.

The mountain resort of Chengde in Hebei province northeast of Beijing has Neolithic origins and a busy history, peopled with various ethnic groups, such as Xiongnu and Mongolians, who led nomadic lives here from the Qin (221 BC-207 BC) to the Ming Dynasty (1368-1644). It became the summer resort capital of the Qing Dynasty (1644-1911) and now is most famous for the Mountain Resort complex of palaces and the Eight Outer Temples to its north, built for the royal families. They spent the hot summer months here in a more welcoming climate and, as well as the mountain scenery, enjoyed the pleasures afforded by the palaces, temples, pavilions, and royal gardens.

North of Chengde is the Puning Temple, a superb blend of Chinese and Tibetan architecture. Built in 1755, it is also called the Big Buddha Temple because of its 73ft (22m) high statue of Buddha, made of pine, cypress, elm, fir, and linden. One of China's largest timber statues, it is blessed with a thousand eyes and arms and represents the bodhisattva of compassion, Guanyin.

The capital of Sichuan is Chengdu, a 2000-year-old city filled with temples, parks, and amazing places to visit nearby, including the Giant Panda Breeding Research Facility and the Buddhist Baoguang Si monastery, founded in the 10th century. It has a 100ft (30m) high pagoda. South of Chengdu at Leshan is one of the most amazing Buddha statues — the world's largest stone statue of Buddha. It was chiseled out of a sheer cliff and, rising 233ft (71m), took 90 years to carve from 713 to 803. It was hoped Buddha's presence would calm the turbulent currents created by the meeting of three rivers here — the Min, Qingyi, and Dadu.

If you have a penchant for the element of water, then Suzhou on the lower reaches of the Chang River is the place to come as some 42 percent of the city is a liquid domain: its patchwork of canals, lakes, ponds, and streams has earned it the name of the 'Oriental Venice.' Here are silk and embroidery factories, temples, and wonderful gardens, including the Garden of the Master of Nets, a United Nations World Heritage site. First constructed over 800 years ago, it was inspired by the lifestyle of a humble fisherman. Today visitors can admire ponds, zigzagging paths, little bridges built of both stone and timber, pavilions, towers, rocky peaks, trees, and flowering shrubs that represent the seasons. It is recognized as being one of the finest gardens in China.

Left: *The modern aspect of Sichuan's capital, Chengdu, a city that dates back at least two millennia and developed from a 4000-year-old Bronze Age culture hereabouts. Today it is home to China's fifth greatest city population (about 10,597,000 people).*

Below: *An old street in Chengdu city that today is a financial hub for West China but is also famous for the making of traditional silk brocade, satin, and the world's first ever paper currency 'Jiao Zi' in 1023.*

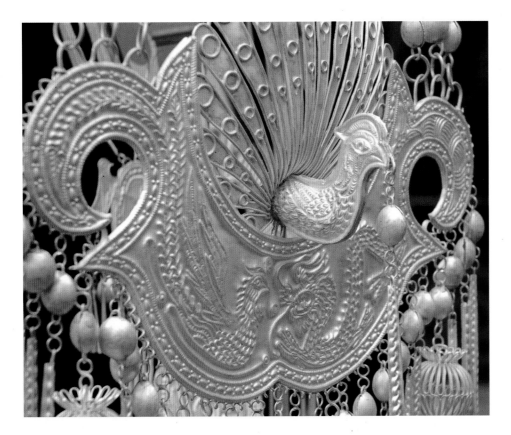

Opposite: The world's largest Dafo (Great Buddha) statue at Leshan, near Chengdu, is a mighty 233ft (71m) high stone sculpture, chiseled out of a cliff and completed in AD 803. It is now a UNESCO World Heritage Site.

Left: Chengdu, gateway to Tibet and the southern Silk Road, is famous for amazing silverwork, like this ornate peacock, and jewelry, as well as silk tapestries and bamboo craftwork.

Below: Dating back to the 400s BC, Suzhou is China's 'Venice,' with a network of canals, streams, bridges, and lakes. It was once a place populated by scholars and merchants and was made prosperous by silk production.

Chinese gardens

In a Chinese garden there are always secrets and surprises around the corner; the aim is to 'change the landscape with every step' so that the scenery mutates and evolves as the visitor walks along and constantly discovers more. There may be a towering rock, a stand of bamboo, or an elegant specimen tree. Doors, galleries, and walls pierced with sculpted windows frame ever-changing vistas while rock gardens, streams, and escarpments contrive to re-create the natural world in miniature. Garden designs have been explored here for over 3000 years — they are sometimes viewed as cosmic diagrams that allow the observer a means of discovering his or her place in the world.

In 2002 scientists found, in a stone slab in northeast China, the fossilized remains of what may be the world's earliest flower: it would have flourished here at least 125 million years ago. Today many of the most popular plants and flowers found in western gardens originated in China. They include a variety of azaleas, camellias, crabapples, chrysanthemums, dianthus, forsythia, flowering almond and peach trees, gardenias, hollyhocks, wisteria, and peonies — China's national flower — to name just a few.

In Sanshui city, Guangdong province, a new 165-acre (66.7ha) Lotus World celebrates this glorious bloom, gathering together most of the identified varieties of the lotus — some 300 or so types.

Opposite: *These gold and silver pagodas in the gardens of Banyan Lake represent the sun and moon. The Sun Pagoda with nine stories is the highest copper pagoda in the world.*

Below: *In Chinese gardens, unanticipated vistas invite discovery. Here the arching shape of a bonsai tree echoes the curves of a quatrefoil doorway, with a glimpse of trellis beyond.*

Background: A cruise ship berths at Harbour City Ocean Terminal in Hong Kong's Victoria Harbour.

Below left: The Bank of China Tower features distinctive triangular patterns in its construction. In 1990, it was the first building outside the United States to top 1000ft (305m).

Below right: The stunning spectacle of Hong Kong's night skyline — thousands of lights glitter around the bay.

Hong Kong

Famous for its cutting-edge steel and glass skyline, Hong Kong offers amazing views — whether seen from land or from out at sea — the element from which many sailors and travelers first gazed at the mix of mountain peaks and stunning buildings as they approached Victoria Harbour. An alternative view became available in 1888, when the Peak Tramway was opened. Tram cars hauled up by 5000ft (1500m) steel cables take passengers up to Victoria Peak, the highest point in Hong Kong at 1811ft (552m). Previously, only a few wealthy residents were able to reach the spot when they were carried there in sedan chairs.

Trips across the harbor on the famous Star Ferry allow another opportunity to absorb the exciting prospects and the spectacle of this incredible modern city is even more stunning at night when thousands of twinkling lights are reflected in the water — laser displays and fireworks sometimes adding to the glamour.

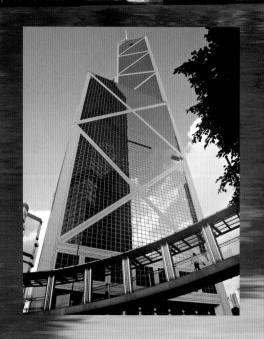

The British occupied Hong Kong in 1841 (following the 1839 First Opium War) and it became a thriving free port and strategic hub for the British Empire, with the addition of the New Territories (Lantau Island and neighboring northern lands) that were granted on a 99-year lease in 1898. It was occupied by the Japanese during World War II and then, in 1997, Hong Kong's sovereignty reverted to China when Britain's administration departed. Despite fears about a possible change of political direction, it remains a beacon of free market and low taxation economics and it continues to develop as a major finance and trade center. It has a population of nearly 7 million, a rich heritage of East-meets-West culture, religious freedom, and a surging economy.

New major bridges here link the urban center to Lantau where the airport is situated: Kap Shui Min, the longest cable-stayed bridge on the globe, Tsing Ma, the world's sixth largest suspension bridge, and Ting Kau, the first major four-span cable-stayed bridge anywhere.

Hong Kong is simply magnificent architecturally. Visitors arriving by air may have their first introduction to China's high-tech modern buildings when they arrive at Hong Kong International Airport designed by Britain's Norman Foster. It opened in 1998 and is lauded for its 'extreme engineering.' Foster was also responsible for the

dramatic exoskeleton trusses and escalator entrance in the 1986 Hong Kong and Shanghai Bank ... but there are so many incredible buildings here, including the Bank of China Tower (opened 1990) with its steel frame and glass curtain wall flaunting gleaming triangle and diamond patterns on the third tallest skyscraper to be found in Hong Kong. The highest is International Finance Centre 2, which has 90 floors; this is the world's seventh tallest office building, its antenna peaking at 1364ft (415.8m). The International Commerce Centre that is presently reaching for the sky in nearby Jiulong will become Hong Kong's tallest building and the globe's fourth tallest tower when completed in 2010.

China has been experiencing an amazing surge in its economy: the Dragon has truly taken off economically in the past two decades with a recent burst of export-led prosperity giving rise to an entirely new image of China, as places like Hong Kong and Shanghai clearly show.

Left: The 1997 Tsing Ma Bridge, which links Tsing Yi island to Ma Wan island over the Ma Wan Channel, is the world's sixth longest suspension bridge and the longest with combined vehicle and rail traffic.

Background: *The amazing skyline of Hong Kong and the sweeping bay — a spectacular view by day or night from Victoria Peak. Some of the world's most expensive properties are located here.*

Right: *The Peak Tramway funicular railroad was opened in 1888 and provided easier access to the elevated viewpoint than the previous stiff climb or ride in a sedan chair.*

Beijing: the capital city

After the international razzmatazz of Hong Kong, it is perhaps fitting to return to China's heritage as discovered most deeply in its capital, Beijing — a city justifiably renowned for its history and culture. An imperial capital since 1279, it has witnessed Mongol Yuan, Ming, and Qing rule and, while it does have the towering skyscrapers and cosmopolitan shopping malls that characterize 21st-century metropolises, it is the old alleyways, gateways, walls, temples, palaces, and beautiful gardens — evoking the very essence of China's past — that most visitors remember.

A city based on a strong geometric design and with many symmetrical features, its core consists of a maze of small alleys (called hutongs), surrounding the royal palace in the Forbidden City. They were built from the Yuan (1279-1368) Dynasty onward. Closest to the palace were the residences of imperial kinsmen and aristocrats while merchants and ordinary folk were housed farther north and south. Almost all lived in homes arranged in sets of four around a quadrangular courtyard with gardens full of date trees, cloves, and pomegranates.

At the heart of it all is the Forbidden City, home to 24 of the Ming and Qing Dynasty emperors. Once heavily guarded, it lies behind a moat and massive wall, overseen by magnificent watchtowers. Built between 1406 to 1420 as a replica of God's Purple Palace, its grand palace housed an emperor regarded as the Son of Heaven. This was the seat of imperial power until 1912 when the Last Emperor abdicated (see page 138). A divine place, entry to which was once forbidden to ordinary people, it is a veritable treasure house, recognized as one of the most important palaces in the world. Not only is it the best preserved imperial palace in China, it is also the largest ancient palatial structure in the world, covering 7,750,000sq ft (720,000m²) and comprising 90 palaces and courtyards, 980 buildings, and 8707 rooms.

Background: An old red door to a forbidden realm — over 500 years ago, Beijing's Forbidden City took four years to build. It was home to 24 Chinese emperors.

Inset above: Various Forbidden City palaces housed the emperor, empress, royal children, officials, and concubines.

Inset right: Pairs of lions guard hall entrances; a lion holds a ball under his paw, a lioness has a cub.

Also at the center of Beijing City is Tiananmen Tower (initially built 1417) and two ancient massive gates. Tiananmen Square, the 'front door' to the Forbidden City is huge, at 108.7 acres (440,000m²), the biggest open town square anywhere in the world. Military displays are held in this vast ceremonial area where a million people can gather. Here too local people relax — often flying kites for their recreation. During celebrations and holidays, it may be covered with fresh flowers. To the square's south side, on the site of the Imperial City's Gate of China, is the Mao Tse-tung Memorial Hall, the resting place of Chairman Mao. His embalmed body, dressed in the familiar gray Mao suit, lies in a crystal coffin.

Some 9 miles (15km) from central Beijing lies the Summer Palace, originally built in 1750 on the site of ancient gardens dating from the 12th century, but which was destroyed by allied British and French troops in 1860. In 1888, Empress Dowager Cixi embezzled navy funds to reconstruct it and now visitors can explore more than 100 royal buildings. A wander along winding paths through the beautiful royal park and classical gardens reveals an

additional wealth of pavilions, towers, bridges, halls, and gateways — set beside tranquil lakes, hills, and dense trees.

The Temple of Heaven in southeast Beijing is enclosed by a long wall, with a semicircular northern part symbolizing the heavens and a southern square section the earth. It covers about 10.4sq miles (27km²). The temple was built (with no nails or pegs) during the Ming Dynasty in AD 1420 for the offering of sacrifices to Heaven, especially on the day of the winter solstice. Connecting the Hall of Prayer for Good Harvest and the Imperial Vault of Heaven is the Vermilion Steps Bridge, along which emperors once believed that they could ascend into Heaven.

Within striking distance of Beijing to the west lies Datong, twice a dynastic capital but now most famous for the spectacular Hanging Monastery at Heng Shan, clinging with impossible tenacity to canyon walls, and the Yungang Caves where 53 caves are the location for 51,000 Buddhist statues. A later collection of incredible statuary also holds court at the Longmen Caves high above the Huang River 7.5 miles (12km) south of Luoyang.

Opposite: Encircled by an artificial lake, Beijing's futuristic National Grand Theater contains an opera house, concert hall, and theater. Locals call this amazing building 'The Egg.' It was designed by French architect Paul Andreu and opened in 2007.

Left: Stairway to the Temple of Heaven ('Tian Tan'), a vast temple complex where imperial offerings and sacrifices were made to the gods during the Ming and Qing Dynasties.

Below: Gate of Heavenly Peace, Tiananmen Square, a Ming Dynasty gate bearing a vast portrait of Mao. It was here that he proclaimed the People's Republic of China in 1949.

The Great Wall

Wall-building began in earnest in China back in the 7th century BC and a new surge in building was experienced from the 5th century BC. The first fortification that used stone as well as earth was built when China was unified in 221 BC. Several walls designed as fortifications, all loosely referred to as the Great Wall, have looped across the landscape through history but it is the historical ruins near Beijing — begun during the Ming Dynasty from 1449 as a defense against Mongol attacks — that are best preserved and the ones most people would recognize as representing the Great Wall.

This is the longest structure ever raised in history, running as it does for some 4000 miles (6400km) along the southern edge of Inner Mongolia — with other branches and secondary sections making a grand total of over 4160 miles (6700km). At its peak, more than one million men guarded this Ming Dynasty wall and some estimates claim between 2 and 3 million Chinese may have died over the long centuries of its construction and defense. It certainly helped to protect the empire against several Manchu invasions but in the end the prohibitive cost of its maintenance and manning, together with power struggles that undermined the existing hierarchy, led to the abandonment of the incredibly ambitious long-term building scheme. Finally one Ming border general, unhappy with his masters, opened the gates to the Manchus in 1644. They promptly seized Beijing, defeated the newly founded Shun Dynasty and launched that of the Qings.

Background: *The Great Wall takes on a golden sheen in the sunset as it loops across the undulating contours of China's hills for thousands of miles, as it has done for some 2200 years.*

Below: *Watchtowers on the Great Wall were systematically spaced no more than two arrow shots apart so that every section of wall could be protected from one vantage point or another.*

Ming and Qing tombs

At Shisanling, some 31 miles (50km) north of Beijing and 15 miles (24km) from the Great Wall is an imperial resting place for Ming emperors. Built between 1409 and 1644, it is approached by the Spirit Way, a long, straight route, flanked by statues — government officials, military officials, and scholars — and animal guards of honor, including lions, camels, horses, elephants, and mythical creatures like unicorns. Beyond lie the remains of 13 of the 16 Ming emperors, 23 empresses, and concubines (some buried alive) in tombs that resemble imperial palaces. The site is feng shui perfection — the peaceful valley is protected on three sides by the Dragon and Tiger mountains that prevent any evil spirits from finding their way in on the north wind.

The Qing Dynasty (1644-1911) rulers are buried in two major sites. The Western Qing Tombs lie 75 miles (120km) west of Beijing and incorporate 14 mausoleums where 78 royals are buried, including four emperors and various empresses, imperial concubines, princes, princesses, and royal servants. The palaces and ancient stone buildings have over 1000 rooms decorated with rich carvings and sculpture.

The Eastern Qing Tombs are found 78 miles (125km) east of Beijing. This is a vast well-preserved tomb complex on Changrui Mountain where five emperors are laid including Emperor Shunzhi (1638-1661), the first Qing emperor, 14 empresses, and many concubines and imperial offspring. Brick paths create sacred ways that connect the tombs in a branchlike arrangement. One of the most elaborate tombs is that of the powerful Empress Dowager Cixi (1835–1908) who never officially ascended the throne but handled affairs of state as a power behind the throne for over four decades. She was one of the most powerful women in Chinese history.

Below: Pairs of elephants, lions, camels, and various mythological beasts join the 'guard of honor' before the Ming tombs at Shisanling — on a site chosen by Ming Dynasty Emperor Yongle in the early 1400s.

Right: This old stone ritual altar is in a Qing Dynasty tomb. The Qing Dynasty lasted from 1644 to 1911 and there are two major mausoleum sites within reach of Beijing — the Western and the Eastern Qing Tombs.

Below: The Dingdongling is the magnificent tomb of the powerful Empress Dowager Cixi (1835–1908), sometimes called the Dragon Lady. One of the Eastern Qing Tombs, it was built before her death at an enormous cost of 72 tons of silver.

Bronze, silver, and gold

As the 21st century gains momentum, the vast Chinese nation — home to 23 percent of the world's population — looks to the future, taking its well-earned place as one of the prime engines of world economy. Just as the awarding of bronze, silver, and gold medals at the 2008 Olympics in Beijing bear witness to an amazing transformation, so does the status of China's economy and industry, reflecting its powerful position on the global stage and rapid rise from ancient culture to modern superpower. China is in the ascendancy … with strengths that permeate all five elements: earth, water, fire, wood, and metal — continuing to influence and direct energy throughout the Land of the Dragon.

Above: Going for gold: Beijing's $400-million Olympic stadium has earned the nickname 'Bird's Nest,' aptly suggesting the interwoven web of twisting steel. The new stadium is able to seat 91,000 spectators and another 30 new sports venues are planned to be erected in the city.

Right: Chinese buildings have been conceived and constructed on an impressive scale for centuries, as this walled fort city of Jiayuguan at the western end of the Great Wall of China bears witness. China is currently experiencing a building boom on an unprecedented scale in human history and, in the process, is using some 36 percent of the world's steel resources.

Fascinating Facts and Figures

Figures do vary, depending on the sources consulted, and some are subject to change, but the following facts provide a fascinating tapestry of China as a nation and a culture.

Land and sea

• At 3,705,676sq miles (9,596,960km²) with a land border of 13,759 miles (22,143km) — when all its disputed territories are included — China is the world's third largest country after Russia and Canada, and the largest entirely in Asia. If disputed territories are excluded, then it ranks fourth on the globe after the United States.

• China is bordered by 14 different countries: Russia, India, Afghanistan, Bhutan, Myanmar, Kazakhstan, North Korea, Kyrgyzstan, Laos, Mongolia, Nepal, Pakistan, Tajikistan, and Vietnam.

• The distance from west to east is about 3231 miles (5200km) and from north to south some 3418 miles (5500km).

• The coastline on the eastern border extends approximately 8700 miles (14,000km).

• Three main seas border mainland China: the Yellow Sea, the East China Sea, and the South China Sea plus the Bohai Sea, which is actually a gulf of the Yellow Sea.

• There are over 5400 islands scattered in the seas off the coast of mainland China.

• China's climate ranges from sub-Arctic in the north to tropical in the south.

• China comprises 22 provinces, five autonomous regions, and four municipalities.

• The Chang is the third longest river on the planet at 3915 miles (6300km).

• China straddles five time zones but has adopted a single standard time: UTC (Coordinated Universal Time, which is Greenwich Mean Time +8 hours).

• The Gobi Desert is the fourth greatest desert of the globe — and Asia's largest. Temperatures here range from 104°F (40°C) to −40°F (−40°C).

• Mount Everest (known as Mount Qomolangma in China) is the highest mountain in the world at about 29,035ft (8850m) in altitude.

• The lowest point in China is Turpan Pendi in the northwest at 508ft (155m) below sea level; only the Dead Sea is lower.

History

• Prehistoric finds in China include Peking man, *Homo erectus*, dating back some 250,000-600,000 years, Yuanmou Man and Lantian Man from between 1 million and 750,000 years ago and the Shu Ape, a primate that dates back some 45 million years.

• China's great civilization dates back some 7000 to 8000 years; this is the world's oldest continuous civilization.

• China has the longest continuously used written language system in the world.

• Chinese astronomers were the first to record a meteoric shower in 2133 BC and a solar eclipse in 1217 BC.

• Once the major highway to and from the east, the Silk Road stretches some 5000 miles (8000km) over land and sea.

• The child Emperor P'u Yi, the last imperial ruler of China from 1908 to 1912, came to the throne when he was only two years old.

• Empress Wu Zetian (625 to 705) of the Tang Dynasty was the only female ruler of China: some claim that she killed two of her sons and a baby daughter in order to achieve her political ambitions. She was certainly ruthless and ambitious but also had a more benevolent side — she set up a scholarly government and instituted fairer taxes.

• China's currency has included cowrie shells (about 3000 to 4500 years ago), bronze pieces (some shaped like spades or knives), the first paper notes (in the 800s), silk notes, and jade. Today the currency is the yuan.

• It took over a million peasants, prisoners, and soldiers to build the Great Wall that was constructed over 1700 years or so to stretch about 1500 miles (2400km) along hill crests on the southern edge of the Mongolian plain.

China today

• The population of China is over 1.3 billion people (1,321,851,000 in July 2007), representing over one-fifth (some 23 percent) of the global population and making it the most populous nation in the world.

• Han Chinese is the largest ethnic group in China (91.9 percent) with the other 8.1 percent made up of 55 official minorities including Zhuang, Uygur, Hui, Yi, Tibetan, Miao, Manchu, Mongol, Buyi, and Korean.

• Mandarin Chinese is the official language of the 206 listed as used in China.

• Religions observed in China include Buddhism that is followed by 1 billion people plus Taoism, Islam, Hinduism, Judaism, Heaven worship, Chinese folk religion, Christianity, and several new religions and sects.

• The 108.7-acre (44-hectare) Tiananmen Square, the original gate to the Forbidden City and Imperial Palace, is the world's largest public plaza, measuring 2887ft (880m) from south to north and 1640ft (500m) from east to west.

• The new Three Gorges Dam is the biggest dam in the world at some 7660ft (2335m) long and 607ft (185m) high. The dam is 377ft (115m) wide at its base and 131ft (40m) wide at the top.

• The Chinese language has over 20,000 characters but most Chinese people will learn only about 5000 of these.

Wildlife and plants

• Over 1000 dinosaur fossils found in Dashanpu, Sichuan province, include four-winged feathered theropods — considered to be the missing link between dinosaurs and birds.

• The earliest flower fossils (125 million years old) were identified here in 2002, discovered in a sand-colored stone slab in northeast China.

• China is home to over 4500 vertebrate species including 1244 bird, 430 mammal, 208 amphibian, 350 reptile, and 2300 fish species.

• Some specimens of the ancient rare ginkgo or maidenhair tree (Ginkgo biloba) here may be up to 3000 years old.

• China has about 46 species of conifers, 33 camellias, 63 hollies, 300 native ferns, 31 magnolias, 66 orchids, 46 rhododendrons, and 58 (21 endemic) species of iris.

• There are more than 574 forest or wildlife natural reserves in China.

• China has 7.4 million acres (3 million hectares) of cultivated paddy fields. Rice may have been grown from circa 9000 BC and domesticated strains were being cultivated by about 6400 BC.

• China is home to 52 out of a world total of 196 species of pheasant in existence.

• The South China tiger (Panthera tigris amoyensis) is perhaps the most critically endangered of the five remaining tiger subspecies in the world.

• Chinese call the rare giant panda the 'bear cat' … perhaps because it is the only bear to have eyes with vertical slit-

Above: Guards on duty at the Gate of Heavenly Peace in Tiananmen Square, Beijing.

shaped pupils (like a cat's eyes) and is also very good at climbing trees.

• The wild yak can survive temperatures as low as −40°F (−40°C), helped by its thick coat, which serves as insulation and blood cells that are about half the size of those of cattle and three times more numerous, so increasing the oxygen levels that its blood can carry.

• The male mandarin duck, revered since the 400s, is often depicted in Chinese art and is a symbol of marital affection and fidelity that is often displayed at wedding celebrations. Pairs of ducks were often presented as gifts to newly-weds.

• The Chinese elephant was extinct by the 14th century BC but today a few Asian elephants roam in a nature reserve in Yunnan province. Local people believe there will be no poverty and unhappiness where elephants live so tolerate their eating of the local rice crops.

Inventions

• The Chinese invented the first ice cream in the 7th century! Other significant inventions include gunpowder, rockets and fireworks, printing, books, papermaking and paper money, the abacus, stirrups, wheelbarrows, seismometers, porcelain, silk, and the compass.

• Chinese medicine includes the practice of acupuncture, an art that has been used here for over 5000 years.

• The Chinese calendar, based on the lunar cycle and comprising 12 Zodiac signs, is the oldest known, originating in 2600 BC. Its complete cycle takes 60 years.

• In China, cars are driven on the right-hand side of the road except in Hong Kong, where the British influence means that they are still driven on the left.

• People have been drinking tea in China for over 1800 years.

• Kung fu was invented by the Shaolin Monks to protect themselves from robbers on the lonely mountain roads.

• Kites were invented sometime between 475 BC and 221 BC — for military purposes. Large wooden ones were used for spying or carrying messages.

China miscellany

• There are 37 million more males than females in China.

• Vast statues in China include Hong Kong's Big Buddha, the world's tallest outdoor seated bronze Buddha. The stone Leshan Buddha is by far the tallest on the planet at 233ft (71m) high and his head is bigger than many a house. There are over 2400 Buddhas carved into the cliffs at Jianjiang Qianfoyan. In Dongfang Fodu Gongyuan (Oriental Buddha Park) is the world's longest reclining Buddha, measuring 558ft (170m) in length.

• More than half a million dollar millionaires are listed as living in China today.

• China's present name derives from the Qin Dynasty (pronounced chin).

• 162 million people use the Internet in China now (2008); there are 2.6 million websites registered in the country.

• Chopsticks were being used during the Shang Dynasty (1562 BC–1066 BC) and have been the utensil of choice since the Han Dynasty (206 BC to AD 220).

• About 440 million people in China currently use cellphones for communicating on the move.

• 'Century eggs' are a delicacy here: the eggs are preserved with special ingredients and buried underground for months before they are uncovered and eaten.

• The Yin-Yang symbol denotes harmony, the meeting point of opposite forces and an eternal cycle as explored in the great book of divination, *I Ching*, (the Book of Changes).

• China's flag is red with one large and four small yellow stars set in the top left-hand corner.

• The dragon is a national icon, and is regarded as an auspicious creature with the power to bless and influence lives. Chinese tradition holds that the people here are descendants of the dragon.

• The four most revered animals of ancient China are the dragon, phoenix (the king of birds), the kylin that, with its dragon head, antlers, horse hooves, ox tail, and wolf forehead, can ward off devils and confer the gift of sons, and — the only 'real' animal — the tortoise, a symbol of longevity and wealth.

• The lion was thought to exorcise evil, bring good fortune, and symbolize power. As well as the renowned lion dance, there are many superb lion sculptures to be found in China in front of important buildings and bridges, palaces, temples and tombs.

Chinese Dynasties

Since imperial dynasties are referred to frequently throughout the text, here is a brief résumé of the relevant dates and their longevity:

Xia 2033 to 1562 BC (471 years)

Shang 1562 to 1066 BC (496 years)

Zhou dynasties 1122 BC to 256 BC (866 years)
    Western Zhou 1066 to 771 BC (295 years)
    Eastern Zhou 770 to 256 BC (514 years)
    (includes Spring and Fall period 770–476 BC, and
    Warring States period 475–221 BC)

Qin 221 to 207 BC (14 years)

Western Han 206 BC to AD 9 (215 years)

Xin AD 9 to 25 (16 years)

Eastern Han AD 25 to 220 (195 years)

Period of Disunity AD 220 to 589
(For 369 years, China is split between several warring kingdoms and ruling houses)

Sui 581 to 618 (37 years)

Tang 618 to 907 (289 years)

Five Dynasties and Ten Kingdoms 907 to 960 (53 years)

Northern Song 960 to 1126 (166 years)

Southern Song 1127 to 1279 (152 years)

Yuan 1279 to 1368 (89 years)

Ming 1368 to 1644 (276 years)

Qing 1644 to 1911 (267 years)

Index